GCSE
Success

Religious
Studies

Dan Phillips
Robert Phillips

Contents

Foundations of Religion

Revised

Religious Practice

Revised

Religious Attitudes

Revised

Ethics

Revised

Judaism and Christianity

Judaism and Christianity

Judaism and Christianity share a common heritage and, as a result, have many practices, scriptures, traditions and holy people in common. Jesus was born a Jew, so it is not surprising that there are similarities.

Judaism looks back to two influential men:
- **Abraham** – the father of the people of Israel
- **Moses** – the founder of the Jewish faith

Judaism: Abraham and Moses

Abraham responded to God's call to leave his home and go to an unknown destination. He travelled from Ur to Haran and then on to **Canaan**.

God's promise to make him the 'father of many nations' is understood to have been fulfilled in the foundation of the people of Israel, the **Hebrew** nation.

Born as a son of a slave in Egypt, Moses was saved from an early death by being hidden in bulrushes by his mother. When he was found and adopted by **Pharaoh's daughter**, his life as an Egyptian prince began.

As an adult, realising the injustice of slavery, Moses killed an Egyptian slave master while defending a Hebrew slave. He became a **fugitive** in a foreign land and encountered God in a **burning bush** who called Moses to return to Egypt to liberate His people.

Pharaoh refused to let the people go and a series of **plagues** were sent by God to 'persuade' him to comply. Following the final plague (the angel of death), Pharaoh decided to allow Moses to lead the Hebrews out of Egypt.

However, Pharaoh changed his mind and pursued the slaves as far as the **Red Sea**. The book of **Exodus** records the miraculous parting of the waves, the escape of the Jews and the death of the ensuing Egyptian army.

During their journey to the Promised Land, God gave Moses the **Ten Commandments**, rules by which to live. After 40 years in the wilderness, the Hebrew people finally entered the Promised Land.

✓ Maximise Your Marks

Abraham's willingness to obey God marked him out as 'God's friend'. If you are able to list examples from his life that illustrate this, such as following God's call to go to a place that he did not know, you will gain higher marks.

✓ Maximise Your Marks

Accuracy is important. Knowing the Ten Commandments and their relevance for today could be useful.

Christianity: Jesus (4 BC–AD 33)

Christianity regards Jesus as its founder. The Gospels of **Matthew** and **Luke** record His miraculous birth to a virgin, Mary. Joseph, Mary's betrothed, was inclined to finish their relationship but Matthew's Gospel tells us that he was dissuaded from this course of action in a dream.

A variety of unusual events, including, stars, angels, shepherds and wise men accompanied Jesus' birth. King Herod tried to have the baby Jesus killed, but the family escaped to Egypt after another warning dream.

Little is known of Jesus' early life as the son of a **carpenter** apart from a visit to Jerusalem when He was 12 years old. Jesus' public **ministry** began when He was about 30. He was baptised in the **River Jordan** by His cousin John the Baptist before spending 40 days and 40 nights in the desert being tempted.

He called 12 men to be His **disciples** to follow and learn from Him. There were fishermen, a tax-collector and a zealot. They stayed with Jesus for about three years.

All four Gospels contain records of Jesus' **teaching** (e.g. the Sermon on the Mount, parables, the 'I am' sayings, etc.) and this teaching is still held in the highest regard by many people today. Christians try to live their lives in accordance with this teaching.

His **miracles** fall into three main categories:
- **healing** miracles and exorcisms
- **nature** miracles
- **resurrections**.

✓ Maximise Your Marks

You should have a detailed knowledge of the key disciples (Peter, James, John, Judas, etc.).

Trial and Resurrection

After about three years of ministry, Jesus and His disciples went to Jerusalem for the **Passover** festival. As He entered the city on a donkey, He was met with public acclaim. The religious authorities, threatened by His success, plotted to have Him put to death. With the agreement of the ruling Roman governor, **Pontius Pilate**, they had Him arrested, tried, convicted and sentenced to death. He was **crucified** on what became known as **Good Friday**.

However, the Gospels record that, when His tomb was visited on the following Sunday morning, His body was gone. This is known as the **resurrection**. The Gospels also record the many accounts of people who claimed to have met with Jesus who, they say, had risen from the dead. Christians call this Sunday **Easter Day** and it is the most important day of the Christian year.

Christians believe in the resurrection but some people do not accept that Jesus rose from the dead. They suggest that the body was stolen or that people saw hallucinations. Many books have been written about this debate and it still provokes much discussion.

? Test Yourself

1 Who visited the baby Jesus in:
   a) Matthew's Gospel and
   b) Luke's Gospel?

2 Who were the main characters in the last week of Jesus' life and why are they important?

★ Stretch Yourself

1 Give five arguments for and against the resurrection of Jesus.

Islam and Sikhism

Islam: Muhammad P.B.U.H. (AD 570–632)

Muhammad was born in **Mecca** (Makkah) in AD 570. Little is known about his childhood except that his parents died when he was young. The fact that he never learned to read and write becomes important when considering his later encounters with the **angel Gabriel**.

Muhammad developed a respect for Judaism and Christianity from an early age and grew up working for his uncle as a shepherd and merchant. His marriage at 25 to a much older widow, **Khadija**, also a merchant, saw him becoming involved in her trading enterprises.

However, dissatisfaction with life in Mecca led him to retreat to the surrounding mountains to meditate. It was in a cave, during the month of **Ramadan** that, at the age of 40, he received the first of his revelations from **Allah**, through the angel Gabriel.

During Gabriel's revelations, Muhammad recited what was revealed until he had learned the information. The core of these revelations was:
- 'God is One' (there is only the One God).
- People must 'surrender' (submit) to Him (literally Islam).
- Muhammad is God's prophet.

Muslims, when using the name Muhammad add the words, 'Peace be upon him' (PBUH).

✔ Maximise Your Marks

Accurate details help to improve your grades. If you can list the details of Muhammad's encounter with the angel Gabriel focusing on what the angel said and how Muhammad remembered it you will gain higher marks.

Gaining Control of Mecca and the Ka'aba

When Muhammad began his public preaching three years later, he attracted few disciples. He encountered hostility in polytheistic Mecca and eventually migrated to **Medina** (Yathrib) in AD 622. This event is known as the **Hijra** and marks the beginning of the Muslim calendar.

During his eight years in Medina, Muhammad's followers grew in number and, on their triumphal return to Mecca, were 10,000 strong. Mecca became monotheistic and the **Ka'aba** became the focus of Islamic pilgrimage.

By the time of his death in AD 632, Muhammad had united the Arabian tribes under one single Muslim banner. After his death, his followers collected his teachings into what became known as the **Qur'an**.

✔ Maximise Your Marks

You will get better marks if you can accurately describe how Muhammad and his followers gained control of Mecca and the Ka'aba. You should also be able to describe the process of collecting Muhammad's teachings into the Qur'an.

Sikhism: Guru Nanak (AD 1469–1539)

Nanak was born near **Lahore** in Pakistan and, from an early age, displayed a keen interest in spiritual matters. This interest was encouraged by family and friends.

When he was 30 he went missing for several days. After reappearing, he began to share his understanding of faith. He said: "There is neither Hindu nor Muslim, so whose path shall I follow? I shall follow God's path."

He went on to explain that, in God's court, God had given him a cup of **nectar** (**amrit**) to drink. His commission was to rejoice in God's name and teach others to do so and Sikhism was born.

Guru Nanak made four major journeys, travelling thousands of miles, spreading his message. He even visited Mecca and Medina, explaining that God was everywhere.

After his death, there were nine other **gurus** who spread and developed the Sikh faith.

✓ Maximise Your Marks

If asked a question about Guru Nanak, explaining what he meant by "There is neither Hindu nor Muslim," will gain higher marks.

Sikhism: Guru Gobind Singh (AD 1666–1708)

Guru Gobind Singh was born as Gobind Rai in Bihar in India, the son of the ninth guru, Guru Tegh Bahadur. He became the tenth guru in 1675, aged nine. He is probably best known for the formation of the Sikh brotherhood, the **Khalsa** in 1699.

Guru Gobind Singh called Sikhs together and demanded sacrificial living from them. The five who responded (the five beloved ones) became the foundation of the Khalsa. He named them 'Singh' (lion) and baptised them. He gave them the **five 'K's** as a sign of their brotherhood:

- **Kesh**: uncut hair
- **Kangha**: a comb
- **Kara**: a steel bracelet
- **Kachha**: practical shorts
- **Kirpan**: a steel sword

These items are very important for Sikhs today.

◊ Boost Your Memory

To help you remember the qualities needed to be a member of the Khalsa, sketch a poster with the title 'The Khalsa needs you'.

❓ Test Yourself

1. How did Allah reveal His message to Muhammad and what did Muhammad do as a result?
2. What are the five 'K's and what do they mean for Sikhs? Think about what they are and how and why they are worn.

★ Stretch Yourself

1. 'Guru Nanak was successful in uniting Muslims and Hindus.' How far is this statement correct? Research the religious situation in Asia and consider the correctness of this statement.

Beliefs

Religious Definitions

Here are some of the main religious definitions that you will find useful.

- **Agnostic** – someone who is not sure whether (or not) they believe in God.
- **Atheist** – someone who does *not* believe in the existence of God or gods.
- **Theist** – someone who *does* believe in the existence of God or gods.
- **Monotheism** – a belief in the existence of *only one* God.
- **Polytheism** – a belief in the existence of *many* gods.
- **Pantheism** – the belief that God is in *everything*.
- **Animism** – the belief that everything has its own in-dwelling *spirit*.

✓ Maximise Your Marks

You will gain higher marks if you can match the major religions to the definitions given above.

Jewish Beliefs

Yahweh is the holiest name that Jews give to God. The **Old Testament** has various other names but this was so holy that the vowels were removed so it could not be spoken. The Book of **Genesis** describes Him as the **Creator** of all things. Jews believe Yahweh to be the one God; all-powerful and all-knowing. Jews consider **Abraham** to be the father of the nation and **Moses** as the founder of their faith.

The most important of all Hebrew texts is the **Torah**, containing, prophecy, poetry, history, a moral code and spiritual guidance. Many Jews believe that there will be a judgement (perhaps after the arrival of the Messiah) resulting in a place in 'heaven' or 'hell'. The spiritual leaders are called **rabbis** and Jews worship on the Sabbath (Saturday) in their holy building, the **Synagogue**.

Christian Beliefs

Jesus Christ (the Messiah), together with the Father and the Holy Spirit are known as the **Trinity**. There is ONE God who reveals Himself in three expressions. God is the Creator of all things but also personal. Christians believe that Jesus perfectly revealed God and that His **death and resurrection** opened the way to forgiveness and eternal life.

In the centuries following the life of Jesus, Christianity spread internationally until it became the official religion of the **Roman Empire** in ad 312 under Constantine the Great.

Christians believe in heaven and hell and that, one day, Jesus will return; the **Second Coming** or **Parousia**. They try to live by the teachings of the Bible, especially the teaching of Jesus and the spiritual guidance in the Letters. Worship, prayer, Bible-study and fellowship are most important and many Christians tithe (i.e. give 10 per cent of their income to charity). The holy day for Christians is Sunday and they worship in a church. Their scriptures are a collection of 66 books making up the Old and New Testament, called the Bible.

✓ Maximise Your Marks

Knowing (and being able to list) how Jews and Christians view scriptures, the Messiah, worship and festivals will gain higher marks.

Islamic Beliefs

Muslims believe that there is only one God, **Allah**, and that He was revealed by **Muhammad** in Arabia 1400 years ago. They consider Muhammad to be the final prophet of Allah, although Abraham, Moses and Jesus are also reverenced as prophets. The teachings of Muhammad were collected into the **Qur'an**.

Muslims believe that, after death, there is a day of judgement with heaven for the faithful and hell for the unbeliever.

The fundamental beliefs are known as the **Five Pillars of Islam**. They are:

- **Shahadah** – the profession of faith
- **Salat** – the ritual prayers, five times daily
- **Zakat** – money for the poor and needy
- **Sawm** – fasting during the month of Ramadan
- **Hajj** – pilgrimage to Mecca

Muslims believe that Allah is eternal and all-powerful and that **submission** to the will of Allah is the main goal for a Muslim. Muslims worship in the **mosque** and Friday prayers are most important.

Sikh Beliefs

Sikhs believe that there is only **one God**; without form or gender. All are equal and all have equal access to God. Consequently, there is no set person in charge of worship.

Although God cannot be fully understood, people can experience 'Him' through worship and devotion. God is within each person but is also external, willing the universe to exist. **Meditating** on God is important and so is doing **good deeds** for others.

Reincarnation is central to Sikh belief and this cycle of birth, life, death and rebirth is a key aspect of the faith. The quality of this existence is dictated by the behaviour of an individual in their previous life. This is known as the Law of **Karma**. Becoming united with God is the only way to break free of this cycle.

There were 10 human gurus, the first of whom was Guru Nanak and the last Guru Gobind Singh. The Sikh holy book is the **Guru Granth Sahib** and is viewed as a living Guru in the world today. Their place of worship is the **gurdwara**. Orthodox Sikhs are easily recognised by the wearing of the **five 'K's**.

This symbol is known as the Khandor and is the symbol of Sikhism.

✓ Maximise Your Marks

Your grade will improve if you can explain the concepts of karma and transmigration of the soul.

❓ Test Yourself

1. What do each of the faiths – Judaism, Christianity, Islam and Sikhism – believe about:
   a) the nature of God?
   b) what happens after death?

⭐ Stretch Yourself

1. Select ONE main belief for Judaism and Christianity and find appropriate texts of scripture to support each belief.

Jewish and Christian Holy Books

The Importance of Holy Books

Each religion has its own Holy Books. They are sometimes known as **scriptures** or 'the Word of God'. Believers often refer to them as being **inspired** and treat them with great respect. Reading from Holy Books takes place in collective worship and/or during an individual's private devotions. They are important to believers for a variety of reasons:

- They teach about the religion's divine being.
- They recount the history of the people and their relationship with their God.
- They provide moral teaching by which to live.
- They offer spiritual guidance.
- They are a vehicle through which God speaks to people today.

Jewish Holy Books

Judaism's 39 books are known as the **Tennakh**, but the five books of the **Torah** are predominant. The five books contained in the Torah are often known as the **Books of Moses** or the **Pentateuch**. They tell the story of:
- Yahweh's creation of all things
- the fall of man
- the beginning of the Covenant
- Moses and the Exodus
- the entry to the Promised Land
- the Ten Commandments and additional laws

There are other books in the collection that are important to Jews.

There are **historical books** that deal with the foundation of the nation of Israel and the establishment of the Monarchy. Books such as Judges 1 and 2 Samuel and 1 and 2 Kings outline the establishment of the nation.

They contain stories about influential characters such as Samson, Saul, David and Solomon.

Books such as Job, Psalms and Proverbs are **Poetic** books. Much of the material in these texts is not only wonderful literature but is used for personal devotion by Jews and Christians alike.

The **Books of the Prophets** are outstanding examples of Yahweh's relationship with His people. Through a variety of individuals (**Amos, Hosea, Isaiah, Jeremiah, Ezekiel** and others) the people were guided and challenged in and through a number of difficult national experiences. Twice the people were taken into exile (Assyria and Babylon) and the message the prophets delivered enabled the people of Israel to be faithful and, later, be restored to their homeland.

The Torah Scrolls

The Torah scrolls are kept in the **Ark** in the synagogue. They are hand-written in Hebrew and are extremely expensive to produce. Each section is written on **parchment** and then glued onto the scroll. If a mistake is made, the whole section has to be rewritten. When being read, the text is never touched by hand, the reading being followed with a **metal pointer** (a **yad**). When the scrolls are removed from the Ark, everyone stands.

At the end of its life, a scroll is not destroyed but given a **ceremonial burial**.

✔ Maximise Your Marks

Research 'the Patriarchs' and the role they played in Israel's early history. Make a list of 10 of the key events in the life of the Hebrew people and why they were important.

Christian Holy Books

The Bible is, in fact, a library of books written by many different men over a long period of time. Altogether, there are 66 books, contained in two separate collections:

- The Old Testament
- The New Testament

The Old Testament is the story of Yahweh's relationship with the people of Israel.

The New Testament is about the coming of Jesus, the Messiah (Christ) and the way that His followers continued His ministry after His death and resurrection. Four of the books, **the Gospels**, relate the birth, life, ministry, death and resurrection of Jesus. Only two of the books, Matthew and Luke, recount the events surrounding the birth of Jesus, Mark's Gospel beginning with the commencement of Jesus' ministry.

These three Gospels, Matthew, Mark and Luke are very similar and are often referred to as the **Synoptic** Gospels. The word 'synoptic' is a combination of two Greek words which mean 'seen together'. They are similar in nature and follow the same basic chronology and pattern, although they each have their own influences, sources and emphases.

The Fourth Gospel and Other Books

The fourth Gospel, the **Gospel of John**, is very different. It appears to be more philosophical and theological than the other three and does not follow the same chronology. The treatment of the miracles and teaching of Jesus is also very different from the other three.

The Acts of the Apostles tells the story of how the disciples spread the Kingdom of God, starting from Jerusalem and then out into the Gentile world. The key characters featured in the book are **Peter**, who was the foundation of the early Church and **Paul** who took the Gospel to the Gentiles.

There are a number of **letters**, or **epistles**, that give guidance to developing congregations. Most of the letters were written by Paul to a variety of churches and individuals in the early years of the Church. There were other letters written by people such as Peter, James and John.

The final book (the **Book of Revelation**) is a mixture of spiritual and moral guidance, prophecy and mystical teaching. It is believed to have been written by the apostle John.

? Test Yourself

1. Who were the main Hebrew prophets and what were their messages about?
2. Who were Peter and Paul?

★ Stretch Yourself

1. What do we know about the four Gospel-writers, the date of their books and their purpose in writing?

Muslim and Sikh Holy Books

Muslim Holy Books

The **Qur'an** contains the 'recitations'. The angel Gabriel (Jibril) appeared to Muhammad and revealed the will of Allah to him. As Muhammad was illiterate, he 'recited' these revelations until he had learned them by heart. The word 'Qur'an' is Arabic and means 'he recited'.

Muhammad collected disciples and relayed these teachings to them. These were memorised by his followers and often written down on scraps of paper, stones and cloth or anything that was to hand. After his death, the first Caliph, Abu Bakr, encouraged Muhammad's followers to collect his teachings together in what is now known as the Qur'an.

Many Muslims consider that the Qur'an is proof of Muhammad's prophethood.

For many years, the Qur'an was hand-written in **Arabic**, but in recent years printing and translation has become common. Despite the Qur'an being **translated** into many languages, Muslims still learn to read and recite it in the original Arabic.

The Qur'an is composed of 114 chapters (or **surahs**). The surahs are not arranged in the order in which they were revealed and vary considerably in length. The longest is nearly 300 verses long whilst the shortest is three.

✔ Maximise Your Marks

Knowing and being able to explain the details of the different stages of the formation of the Qur'an will gain higher marks.

Respecting the Qur'an

Because Muslims believe the Qur'an to be the inspired word of Allah, it is treated with the greatest **respect**. There are various ways in which Muslims show respect to the Qur'an:
- washing before handling the book
- keeping it in a cloth when not in use
- storing it in a clean, appropriate place
- placing it on a higher shelf than any other book
- not speaking, eating or drinking whilst it is being read
- being on your best behaviour in its presence

One of the greatest marks of respect a Muslim can show is to **memorise** the Qur'an. A person who does this is known as a '**hafiz**'.

Muslim children learn to read the Qur'an in Arabic from an early age.

✔ Maximise Your Marks

You will gain higher marks if you can accurately relate how Muslims show respect for the Qur'an.

Sikh Holy Books

The **Guru Granth Sahib** is a collection of teachings and hymns written by a variety of Sikh leaders over many years. The first guru was **Guru Nanak** and his hymns and teachings were written down by the second guru, **Guru Angad**. Other gurus to contribute to the scriptures were:

- Guru Amar Das
- Guru Ram Das
- Guru Arjan

Eventually the tenth guru, **Guru Gobind Singh**, added the hymns of his father Guru Tegh Bahadur, resulting in what is now known as the **Guru Granth Sahib**. He decreed that, after his death, there should be no more human gurus: the Guru Granth Sahib should take their place as the 'living' Guru. Sikhs do not usually keep copies of the Guru Granth Sahib in their homes. As it is believed to be a living Guru, it is treated with the same respect as any of the other gurus would receive if they were alive.

Respecting the Guru Granth Sahib

All copies of the Guru Granth Sahib are **identical in layout**. There are 1430 pages and every verse is in the same place on the same page. This attention to detail is just one example of the way that Sikhs treat their scriptures with **respect**.

Other examples of respect are:
- bathing before handling the book
- keeping it in its own room when not in use
- covering it in silk cloth
- carrying it above the head when moving it

- bringing it gifts in worship
- reading it before making important decisions
- marrying before it

The Guru Granth Sahib is vital for Sikhs because they believe that it contains the words spoken by their gurus who were revealing the word of God (Waheguru). Consequently, the book is central to every act of worship in a gurdwara. Indeed, a building cannot be a gurdwara unless it has at least one copy of the Guru Granth Sahib.

❓ Test Yourself

1. How do the following religions show respect to their holy books?
   - **a)** Jews
   - **b)** Christians
   - **c)** Muslims
   - **d)** Sikhs

⭐ Stretch Yourself

1. Imagine you were a Jew, Christian, Muslim or Sikh and explain to someone not of your faith:
   - **a)** why your holy book is important to you and
   - **b)** how you show it respect.

The Gospels

What are the Gospels?

The word 'gospel' means '**good news**'. For Christians, the good news concerns the birth, life, example, death and resurrection of Jesus. Several decades after the events, Christians collected **eye-witness** accounts (their own and others') and compiled them into books about Jesus, known as **Gospels**.

There were numerous Gospels but only four found their way into the **New Testament**:
• Matthew
• Mark
• Luke
• John

Matthew

Although Matthew's appears first in the New Testament, it was not the first to be written. That was probably the Gospel of Mark. Most commentators agree that the author of Matthew's Gospel used Mark as a source, together with other sources. It has **Jewish** influences and appears to be written for Jewish readers by a Jewish Christian in the first century. The author is keen to show that Jesus was the long-awaited Messiah and that He was a true descendant of Abraham. Wise men seeking Jesus are only found in this Gospel. The **Sermon on the Mount** is found in this book.

The Gospel was probably written in Syrian Antioch, about AD 80.

Luke

Luke wrote two books that feature in the New Testament – the Gospel and the **Acts of the Apostles**. He was a Gentile and he was not an eye-witness to the events of the life of Jesus. Both volumes are dedicated to an individual, **Theophilus**, although the name may simply mean 'God-lover'.

It is commonly held that Luke wrote his Gospel for **Gentile** readers. There are frequent explanations of Hebrew terms and practices and the line of Jesus is traced all the way back to Adam. It is this Gospel that has the birth stories involving the shepherds.

The Gospel was probably written about AD 85 but there is no consensus of location.

Mark

Considered by most to be the first Gospel to be written. Many commentators think that the author was an eye-witness, possibly the young man almost arrested after the Last Supper. The gospel is the shortest of the four and gives the impression of **urgency**. There are no **birth stories**, as in Matthew and Luke, and the **resurrection accounts** are shorter than in the other Gospels. Because of this abrupt ending, it is suggested that the original end of the Gospel was lost. It may have been written in Rome about AD 65.

⚲ Boost Your Memory

To help you remember facts relating to the Gospel writers (such as influences, sources, dates, audience and special features), draw a 'spider chart' for each of the writers.

John

John's Gospel was the last to be accepted into the New Testament and is very different from the other three. It has far less biographical material and the style of teaching he records has few similarities to that in the other three. Gone are the short, vivid parables; long discourses and **'I am' sayings** have taken their place. Only **seven miracles** are recorded and they are seen as **'signs'**.

This Gospel is considered to be the most **theological** and **philosophical** of the four.

It is believed that it was written in Ephesus, probably in the late AD 90s.

The Synoptic Question

The important question is: 'Why are three of the Gospels so similar to each other and so different from the fourth?' The word 'synoptic' literally means **'to see together'**. The most popular solution is as follows:

- Mark's Gospel was probably the first to be written, based on **eye-witness testimony** and the teaching of **Peter**.
- Matthew and Luke used Mark's Gospel as a basic source and then added their own individual sources and eye-witness accounts. It is interesting that they follow his basic chronology and that when they differ from it they rarely do so at the same time.
- Matthew and Luke also used a **common teaching source** (known as **'Q'**) that contains material not in Mark's Gospel. Much of the material in the Sermon on the Mount (Matthew) and the Sermon on the Plain (Luke) comes from this source.

- The fourth Gospel is believed to be so different because it comes from a different **tradition** and a much later date (or much earlier date) from the other three. Traditionally the date of composition has been considered to be late. Conversely, some recent scholarship has suggested that it may have been the first to be written.

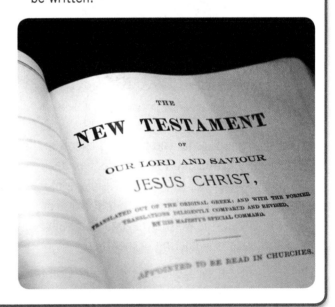

❓ Test Yourself

1. Who were the main sources for the Gospels of Matthew, Mark and Luke?
2. How is the start and end of Mark's Gospel so different from that of Matthew and Luke?
3. What is the evidence for the existence of the source 'Q'?

⭐ Stretch Yourself

1. Explore how cultural and religious influences had an effect on the Gospel writers and on the Gospels that they wrote.

Jewish and Christian Holy Buildings

Foundations of Religion

Why Holy Buildings are Important

All religions have places where they **congregate** to worship together. There are a variety of reasons why they are important:

- In order that the congregation may feel safe and secure.
- To provide security for holy books and valuable artefacts.
- To protect against the weather.
- So that external distractions can be avoided.

- To create a space which is different and special.
- So that worshippers can be quiet if they want to be.

However, holy buildings are not just for worship. They are places where believers can meet and share in friendship and fellowship. They are often places of study. Many are centres for **community** activity and it is common for them to be a focus of support for families of all ages.

Jewish: The Synagogue

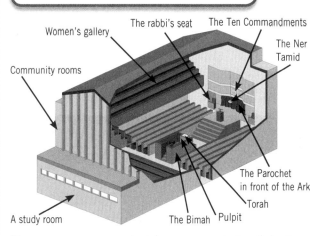

Women's gallery — The rabbi's seat — The Ten Commandments — The Ner Tamid — Community rooms — The Parochet in front of the Ark — Torah — A study room — The Bimah — Pulpit

The synagogue or **schul** (pronounced shool) is the special place of worship for Jews. As has been previously suggested, it is not just a place of worship but also a meeting place and place of study. In Greek, the word 'synagogue' literally means a place of gathering or meeting.

The focus of the synagogue is the **Ark** containing the **Torah scrolls**. The Ark is a cupboard, elaborately carved and often gilded with Hebrew words and letters, which contain the scrolls belonging to the synagogue. Each scroll is **hand-written** and is extremely expensive. When the doors of the Ark are open, all present stand as a mark of respect. To read from a scroll, it is carried to the **Bimah** (the raised platform) and placed on the **pulpit** (reading desk). The text of the scrolls is never touched by hand but a metal pointer (**a yad**) is used to follow the reading.

There is usually a traditional seven-branched **menorah** which is now the emblem of the modern state of Israel.

Close to the Ark is a copy of the main Hebrew words of the **Ten Commandments** and above it is the **Ner Tamid** (the Eternal Light). This represents the presence of God and recalls the light kept burning in the Temple and the pillar of fire that guided the travelling Jews.

In front of the Ark hangs the **Parochet** (curtain) representing the original cover for the Ark of the Covenant. This is often highly decorated and could contain the **Star of David**, also commonly seen in synagogue windows or displayed outside.

In Orthodox synagogues, worship will be in **Hebrew** and the unaccompanied singing led by a **cantor** (song leader). Traditionally, men and women **sit separately** but, in a Reform synagogue, they often sit together. Before worship can begin, there must be a **minyan** (a minimum of 10 adult male Jews). Heads must be covered as a sign of respect and a **Tallit** (prayer shawl) worn for morning prayers.

✓ Maximise Your Marks

If you can describe the origin of and meaning for each of the symbolic objects you will gain higher marks.

Christian: The Church

Traditionally, **Anglican** churches are built in the shape of a cross (**cruciform**) and face East (towards Jerusalem) when looking towards the altar. However, there are many variations on this and churches can be built in any shape and may face in any direction. The **symbolism** of the various objects inside the church helps to explain the attitude of believers to their faith:

- **The font** is the vessel that holds the holy water for **baptism**. It is through baptism that a person first gains entry to the fellowship of the church. The symbolism of locating it by the **entrance** is to remind people of this. In non-conformist churches and chapels, this is not the case. Less emphasis is given to the font and it is usually found near the front.
- **The aisle** symbolises the believer's **journey** of faith towards God.
- **Pews** were intended to be uncomfortable to help worshippers to concentrate.
- **Stained glass windows** were very important as **illustrations** of the Bible stories in a time when most people were illiterate. They were often memorable visual aids for the Gospel message.
- **The altar** is very important in Anglican and Catholic churches, emphasising the centrality of the **bread and wine** (body and blood of Jesus) in worship. It is usually the highest place in the church and has a cross or crucifix on it. It is here that the 'elements' (bread and wine) are blessed and distributed.
- **The pulpit** is the raised area from which the preacher will deliver the **sermon**. In non-conformist churches, this can often be in the middle rather than at the side. This change of location displays a difference of emphasis: the 'preaching of the Word' being of more importance than the 'breaking of bread'.

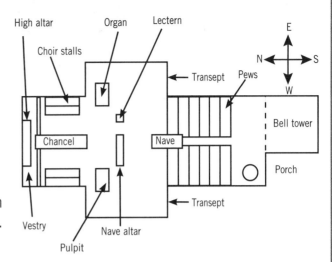

- **The lectern** is a reading desk from which the Bible is read. It is often carved in the shape of an eagle.
- A **holy water stoup** can be found inside the entrance of Catholic churches so that worshippers can 'sign' themselves with the cross as they come in. They also bow before the altar.
- **Candles** are very common and symbolise the presence of God and that Jesus is the Light of the World.

Different **denominations** have different attitudes to symbolism in the worship area. Some are very plain with little by way of symbolism. Others are very elaborate. This difference reflects the way that different congregations approach worship.

Foundations of Religion

✓ Maximise Your Marks

To gain a higher mark, you need to be able to list the different objects found in a church and explain their symbolic meaning.

❓ Test Yourself

1. List the main symbolic objects in:
   a) a synagogue
   b) a church

⭐ Stretch Yourself

1. Explain the symbolic significance of three symbolic objects in:
   a) a synagogue
   b) a church

Muslim and Sikh Holy Buildings

Muslim: The Mosque

The mosque is a '**place of prostration**'. Before entering the mosque, shoes are removed and placed in a **rack** and heads covered. There are different entrances for men and women and, inside the prayer hall, they sit separately. This is for modesty reasons. (Women do pray in the mosque but it is more common for them to pray at home.) Muslims then perform **wudu** – ritual washing before entering the prayer hall. There is a special area for this to take place.

- A – **The mihrab** is a niche in the wall which shows the believer the direction of Mecca, towards which Muslims pray.
- B – **The minaret** is a tower from which the **Call to Prayer** is issued. The **muezzin** calls the faithful to prayer five times a day.
- C – **The mimbar** are the **steps** from which the **Imam** preaches.
- D – **The dome** above the main prayer room which represents the **Universe**.
- E – **The zulla** is the main prayer room. It is bare, with no furniture – the worshippers sitting on the floor to show the equality of all Muslims. There are no pictures and statues on view because they are considered to be blasphemous.

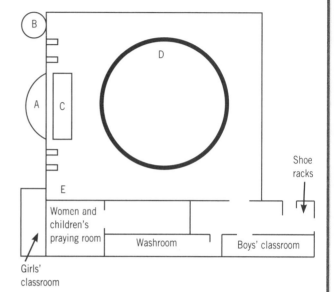

Each mosque has its own classrooms where children go to learn **Arabic** so that they can read the Qur'an. Lessons take place in the evening after school. They are also taught the **Raka'ah** (the ritual prayer positions).

In non-Muslim countries, mosques may not always have a minaret because the Call to Prayer may not be broadcast publically but issued internally.

✔ Maximise Your Marks

You will gain higher marks, if you can accurately describe a visit to the mosque, beginning with the Call to Prayer and ending with the departure.

Sikh: The Gurdwara

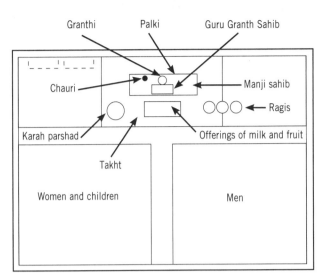

The gurdwara is the place where Sikhs **congregate** for worship and literally means the 'residence of the Guru'. A building is only a gurdwara if it contains a **Guru Granth Sahib**. The gurdwara is not just a place of worship but somewhere that Sikhs may **learn**, **ceremonies** can be undertaken and a place of **service** for the community. The focus of all worship is the Guru Granth Sahib as can be seen by its treatment by Sikhs.

- Most people attend the gurdwara on a **Sunday**, although Sikhs can attend any day.
- Outside each gurdwara a **flag** is flown bearing the Sikh emblem.
- Before entering the gurdwara, Sikhs **remove their shoes** and cover their heads.
- There are **four doors** into a gurdwara, symbolising that people from all four points of the compass are welcome.
- Each gurdwara has a **special room** where the Granth is kept when not in use. It is common for it to be kept in a bed at night.
- In the main hall, the Granth is placed on the **Takht** (raised platform), under a canopy (**Palki**). It is here that the **granthi** reads from the book.

- To the side of the Takht is a place for the **ragis** (musicians) who will accompany parts of the worship.
- On entering, Sikhs **bow** before the book, touching the floor with their foreheads, symbolically showing their obedience. **Offerings** are placed before the Guru Granth Sahib.
- There are no seats in the hall and Sikhs **sit on the floor** with feet pointing away from the book.
- Men and women **sit on separate sides of the hall**.
- All worship concludes with the sharing of **Karah Parshad** (the ritual pudding).
- Every gurdwara has a **Langar** where the communal meal is served, to which all are welcome.

✓ Maximise Your Marks

Describe how a gurdwara reflects the Sikh attitude to the Guru Granth Sahib. List each of the attitudes and relate them to the building. Accurate details attract better marks.

❓ Test Yourself

1. List the main symbolic elements in each of the following:
   a) the mosque
   b) the gurdwara

⭐ Stretch Yourself

1. Why is symbolism important in places of worship?

Practice Questions

Complete these exam-style questions to test your understanding. Check your answers on page 90. You may wish to answer these questions on a separate piece of paper.

1 Describe the main features of a Christian place of worship and explain their importance. (5)

2 Describe the different parts of the Bible and what their purpose is. (5)

3 Explain why knowing how a religion was founded is important to one of its members. (5)

4 Explain how a holy book is significant to a religious believer. (5)

5 Explain why the Gospels may provide different accounts of the same events. (5)

....

....

....

....

....

6 For all of the following questions, explain whether you agree with the statement. You must then give reasons to support your answer and show that you have thought about different points of view. You must refer to the teachings of at least one religion in your answer.

a) "No one religion has got it right; we are all climbing the same mountain." (4)

....

....

....

....

....

b) "My religion's book is the Word of God, so I must believe every word of it." (4)

....

....

....

....

....

c) "I don't need to go to a holy building to worship my God." (4)

....

....

....

....

....

How well did you do?

| 0–21 | Try again | 22–26 | Getting there | 27–31 | Good work | 32–37 | Excellent! |

Jewish and Christian Worship

What is Worship?

All religions express the 'worth' that they place in their God or gods. They do so in a variety of ways. The main thing that they have in common is that they want to **communicate** with their deity in a way that shows how important He/they are to them.

Definition of **WORSHIP**:
- **reverence** offered to a divine being or supernatural power
- an act of **expressing** such reverence
- collective or individual **adoration** directed towards a deity

Worship is expressed in a variety of ways. Each faith has its own particular emphases and practices, but there are some elements of worship that are common to all faiths. Prayer, reading scriptures, singing devotional songs, fasts and festivals, sharing food, chanting and dance are a few of many such elements. Most worship is conducted in designated buildings such as a synagogue, church, mosque or gurdwara.

Religious Practice

Jewish Worship

Jews meet for collective worship in a synagogue on the **Sabbath** (Friday sunset to Saturday sunset). The service is led by a **rabbi** and the singing by a **cantor** (song leader). The central part of the service is the reading from scripture.

In order for the **Torah** to be taken out of the **Ark** and read in worship, there has to be a **minyan** (a minimum of 10 adult male Jews). All stand when the Torah is removed from the Ark and taken to the **Bimah** (reading desk).

Readings from the scriptures, prayers, singing psalms and a sermon usually make up the main elements of worship.

The service is conducted in Hebrew and the cantor will lead the singing without musical accompaniment. In orthodox synagogues, men and women are separated either by a screen or a balcony. Hats are commonly worn in worship as a sign of respect. Men usually wear a **yarmulke** (a small round cap) and a **Tallit** (prayer shawl).

✓ Maximise Your Marks

You will gain higher marks if you know why the location of the Bimah in a synagogue is significant. (Think about the importance of the Torah.)

Meals and Jewish Worship

Many elements of Jewish worship are based in the home, such as the Sabbath meal. The ritual in the meal is an integral part of worship. The celebration of various festivals is also centred in the home. The Passover meal is a good example of this.

Christian Worship

Christian worship has its origins in Hebrew worship, so it is not surprising that there are a number of similarities. Reading from the scriptures, prayers, songs and a sermon are most common. Christians worship together on **Sunday** and meet in a **church**. Sunday is important because of Jesus' resurrection. It is the day of the week when Jesus was resurrected.

It is common for a priest, vicar or minister to lead worship, although it is not unusual for non-ordained people to lead worship in several **denominations**. Within the Christian church, there is a wide variety of different approaches to worship. Some focus on reading and understanding the Bible, others the receiving of bread and wine in **Holy Communion** (**Eucharist**) and yet others in quiet **meditation** and prayer.

Where receiving the bread and wine is central, the focus in worship is on Jesus' last supper and His death and resurrection. Special emphasis is given to the mystery of receiving Jesus through His body and blood (bread and wine). The priest/vicar will distribute the '**elements**' and the congregation will kneel or stand at the communion rail to receive them. Worship will also contain hymns and songs, prayers, Bible-readings and a sermon.

In worship where the Bible is central, there is much more emphasis on reading scripture and explaining its significance for the believer. This explanation is known as a **sermon**. In a sermon, the preacher will explore how Christians should live their lives in relation to what the Bible teaches. Special emphasis is placed on the life, teaching, death and resurrection of **Jesus**.

✓ Maximise Your Marks

What does the location of the altar and the pulpit tell us about the different emphases in worship in different denominations? Think about the altar (bread and wine) and the pulpit (preaching). Whatever the focus of worship, the congregation is encouraged to fully participate by singing, praying, listening and reading. In different traditions, people might also kneel, bow, raise their hands, clap or dance.

Confession

In the Roman Catholic denomination, there is special focus on '**confession**'. Members of the congregation will visit the priest privately in order to confess their sin and ask for forgiveness.

When they confirm that they are truly sorry, the priest will offer forgiveness and confer a '**penance**' (a task to show sincere repentance).

❓ Test Yourself

1. What are the main elements of worship found in each of the faiths outlined above?

2. List the differences and explain why they are different.

3. Who leads worship in each faith and why is one different from the others?

⭐ Stretch Yourself

1. Compare Jewish worship with what goes on in Christian worship. What are the similarities? What are the differences? How would you explain those similarities and differences?

Muslim and Sikh Worship

Religious Practice

Muslim Worship

Muslims hold their main act of collective worship in a **mosque** on a Friday. Muslim worship is dominated by prayer, both in the mosque and at home. Before entering the mosque, Muslims must remove their shoes and carry out ritual washing (known as '**wudu**').

Five times each day, Muslims are called to prayer from the **minaret** by the **muezzin**. If a Muslim is not able to attend the mosque for prayer, they may pray in a clean, appropriate place on a prayer mat facing Mecca. This ritual prayer (**Salat**) is one of the Five Pillars of Islam and occurs at:

- dawn
- midday
- late afternoon
- sunset
- between sunset and midnight

While saying prayers, there are a series of special movements known as **Rak'ah**. These prayer positions are common to both private and public prayer. The different positions have a relevance to the prayers being prayed.

Friday Prayers

Friday prayers (the **Jumu'ah**) are the most important of the week, although prayers occur in the mosque throughout the week. They take place soon after noon, after the muezzin issues the call to prayer from the minaret. Male Muslims must attend Friday prayers; women may attend but often pray at home. In the prayer hall, which is without furniture or pictures, there is a niche in the wall, called a **mihrab**. This clearly shows the direction of Mecca, towards which Muslims must face when they pray.

During Friday prayers, led by the Imam, the **Qur'an** will be read, a sermon preached and the ritual prayers undertaken. At the end of these prayers, **Zakat** is collected. This giving to the poor is not a good-will gift but a systematic collection of 2.5 per cent of one's wealth. Zakat is one of the Five Pillars of Islam.

Sikh Worship

Sikhs can worship in private or publically together.

Privately, a Sikh wakes early, bathes and begins the day by **meditating** on God. There are set prayers that a Sikh should recite in the morning, the evening and before going to sleep. The wearing of the **five 'K's** is a daily public demonstration of the Sikh's worship and devotion.

Any Sikh, male or female, can lead worship in a **gurdwara**. Before coming into the presence of the book, Sikhs must remove their shoes and cover their heads. Cigarettes and alcohol must be removed before entering. On entering the main hall, Sikhs bow before the **Guru Granth Sahib** which has been brought from its own room and placed on the **takht** (raised platform). The book is covered with silk cloth while it is not being read and the **granthi** will wave a **chauri** (fan) over the book when it is. The granthi is an ordinary Sikh who has been trained to read the scriptures and organise worship. Offerings of food and money are placed before the Guru Granth Sahib before each person sits on the floor with their feet facing away from the book. Men and women sit separately. All this is symbolic of the respect shown to the contents of the book.

Sikh Services

There is no specific holy day but most services in England are on Sunday.

A typical service will contain readings from the Granth, singing hymns (accompanied by musical instruments), prayers and a sermon. At the end of the service, **Kara Parshad** (sacred food) is shared by all. It is a sweet made from wheat flour, sugar and clarified butter. Non-Sikhs are welcome to share in worship but they are expected to submit to the same code of conduct as a Sikh. A service could last for several hours and worshippers don't always stay for the whole service. However, they are encouraged to at least be present at the beginning and the end.

At the end of worship everyone attends a simple fellowship meal called the **Langar**. This is also the name for the place where the food is served. Although Sikhs are not expected to be vegetarian, only vegetarian food is served in the Langar so that anyone can attend.

✓ Maximise Your Marks

Make a detailed list of what takes place during a Sikh act of worship. Accurate details attract higher marks.

❓ Test Yourself

1 What are the main elements of worship found in Islam?

2 What preparations must a Muslim make?

⭐ Stretch Yourself

1 If a Sikh were planning the worship in the gurdwara, what elements would they include and why would they be included?

Attitudes to Prayer

Religious Practice

Jews at Prayer

Prayer (public and private) is an essential part of a Jew's faith and should be practised three times a day: morning, afternoon and evening. Prayer can be extemporary (made up) or can be read from a book. Like most believers, Jews tend to use both.

Thanksgiving (expressing gratitude), praise (showing approval of who God is and what He does) and petition (asking for things) are the most common forms of prayer. Jews believe that, when they pray, they become closer to God and more able to understand and obey His will for their lives.

The siddur (the Jewish prayer book) contains services which help with the discipline of regular prayer. It contains patterns of prayer taken from the writings of great Jews throughout history.

Praying at the Western Wall

When praying, a Jew will cover their head and wear a prayer shawl. The shawl (**Tallit**) has fringes and knots which remind the wearer of the 613 laws found in the **Torah** and their responsibility to be obedient. When praying at the **Western Wall** in Jerusalem, people can be seen slipping written prayers into the cracks and crevices between the stones.

This is because the Western Wall is the last remaining wall of the Great Temple. For Jews, it is the holiest place in their religion and they believe that by putting prayers in between the stones of the wall they are communicating directly with God.

✓ Maximise Your Marks

Find examples of prayer from the siddur and collect them under the headings: thanksgiving, praise or petition. Remember, accuracy matters.

Christians at Prayer

Prayer is an essential part of every public act of worship and is seen as being '**in conversation**' with God. Many Christians like to spend a part of each day in private prayer as well as praying together in church.

The Lord's Prayer

The **Lord's Prayer** is considered to be the most important Christian prayer. This is because Christians believe it comes directly from Jesus and they are praying as He taught them to do. Some believe it should be repeated exactly as found in the New Testament or some other modern version of it. Others consider it to be a template for prayer and use each part of it as a type of heading. However Christians pray, it is the sincerity of the prayer that is important.

Many people find it helpful to kneel or close their eyes when praying. Others can be seen with their faces uplifted and their hands open. There is no set process.

⚲ Boost Your Memory

The acronym **ACTS** is often seen as being helpful. It stands for:
- Adoration – telling God how wonderful He is.
- Confession – saying sorry for wrong-doing and asking for forgiveness.
- Thanksgiving – showing gratitude for who God is and what He has done.
- Supplication – asking God to meet our needs and the needs of others.

Muslims at Prayer

Muslims pray five times every day. This is called **Salat** and is one of the **Five Pillars of Islam**. Prayers are said at dawn, midday, late afternoon, sunset and late evening. In Muslim countries, the **Call to Prayer** will alert the believer of the correct time. These prayers are accompanied by ritual movements called the **Rak'ah**. These movements relate directly to the particular element of prayer being said.

When a Muslim prays outside the mosque, they use a **prayer mat**, set out to face Mecca. This must be in a clean, appropriate place. If a prayer mat is not available, the Muslim should still pray. Solo prayer is important but collective prayer in the mosque is better.

Praying at the Mosque

When praying in a mosque, the **Imam** leads the prayers. Before entering to pray, Muslims remove their shoes, cover their heads and perform **wudu** (ritual washing). Whilst praying, Muslims face the **mihrab**, a niche in the wall denoting the location of Mecca. Although women can pray in the mosque, it is more common for them to pray at home.

✓ Maximise Your Marks

Knowing the words of 'the call to prayer' and the five times of the day it can be heard, and using this information appropriately in your exam, will gain higher marks.

Sikhs at Prayer

Perhaps the most important prayer is the **Ardas**. It is in three parts:
- Part 1 – **meditation** on the Almighty and contemplation of the Gurus.
- Part 2 – remembering the **sacrifices** of Sikhs throughout history.
- Part 3 – **supplication** and asking for forgiveness.

The Ardas is always said before moving or opening the **Guru Granth Sahib** and is used during every important occasion.

Although Sikhs have set times of the day for prayer in the **morning** and the **evening**, they consider that prayer should be continuous throughout the day. Everyday actions and service should be part of prayer. True prayer is a channel between the believer and God and is a source of **grace** from God. The greater the **humility**, the greater is the flow of grace.

It is not surprising that prayer plays such a big part in the life of a Sikh as much of the Guru Granth Sahib is composed of collections of prayers. In Sikhism, anyone can pray.

? Test Yourself

1. List the different *types* of prayer and explain how they are used.

2. Why is prayer important for the believer?

★ Stretch Yourself

1. How would a member of each of the above faiths answer these questions?
   a) When do they pray?
   b) Where do they pray?
   c) Why do they pray?

Pilgrimage

Embarking on a Pilgrimage

When believers embark on a pilgrimage, they are not going on holiday. They are visiting a holy place that, in their faith, has a special significance. The place may be significant for various reasons:

- It may be the place of a **founder's birth**.
- The founder may be **buried** there.
- A **major event** in the history of the religion may have happened there.
- It may have a connection with an **important member** of the faith.

Jewish Places of Pilgrimage

Jerusalem
For many centuries, Jerusalem has been the centre of faith for all Jews. Until its destruction in AD 70, adult male Jews were required to visit the **Temple** and offer sacrifices, especially during **Passover**. Following the **diaspora** (the scattering of the Jews), pilgrimage to Jerusalem was largely discontinued.

Since 1967, the remaining wall of the Temple (the **Western Wall**) has, once again, become the most sacred site for devout Jews. Prayers and Bar Mitzvahs at the Wailing Wall are most important.

Jerusalem is also important for Christians and Muslims. The **Dome of the Rock** is one of Islam's most important shrines and there are a number of important churches associated with the **death and resurrection** of Jesus.

Pilgrimage to Jerusalem is not compulsory and there are other sites that Jews visit, such as **Masada**, the Holocaust memorial (**Yad Vashem**) and **Mount Sinai**.

✓ Maximise Your Marks

Being able to recount a detailed list of what a Jew might see and do when visiting the Western Wall could help to gain better marks.

Christian Places of Pilgrimage

Israel
Many Christians visit places that were important in the **life of Jesus**. Bethlehem, Nazareth, the Sea of Galilee and Jerusalem are very popular.

Rome – St Peter's Basilica
The centre of the **Roman Catholic Church**, Rome, is visited by millions of Catholic Christians each year. The remains of St Peter are believed to be buried here. The **Vatican** is the home of **the Pope**.

France – Lourdes
The waters of Lourdes are believed to bring **healing** and millions of Christians seek healing there every year. It is special because the **Virgin Mary** is believed to have appeared to a young girl called **Bernadette** in 1858.

England – Canterbury and Walsingham
Both are minor places of pilgrimage for English Christians. Canterbury is important because of the martyrdom of **Thomas Becket**. Walsingham became important following a vision of the Virgin Mary to **Richeldis de Faverches** in 1061 and the building of a replica of Mary's house in Nazareth.

Scotland – Iona
A monastery was built here following the arrival of **Columba** in AD 530, who brought Christianity to Scotland from Ireland. Pilgrimage to these sites is not compulsory.

Sikh Places of Pilgrimage

It was felt that, like other faiths, Sikhs needed a holy place in which to worship and so **Guru Arjan** developed earlier work by initiating the building of the **Golden Temple in Amritsar**. The work began in December AD 1588 and was completed in AD 1604. The Temple is surrounded by a large lake which was created earlier.

Pilgrimage to the Temple is not compulsory but it is regularly visited by Sikhs from all over the world.

Muslim Places of Pilgrimage

Mecca – Hajj
At least once in their life, every Muslim must undertake pilgrimage to **Mecca**. If they cannot (e.g. for health reasons), they can pay someone else to undertake it for them. If needed you can also pay someone to take your ashes after your death. This is known as **Hajj** and is one of the **Five Pillars of Islam**.

There are a number of stages:
- **Ihram** – before beginning the Hajj, Muslims must purify themselves (wearing two white cloths).
- On entering Mecca, **Tawaf** (circling the **Ka'aba** seven times) is undertaken. Pilgrims then travel between **Safa** and **Marwa** seven times commemorating Hagar's desperate search for water for her son, Ishmael. Pilgrims then go to Mina and spend a day there.

- Following morning prayers in Mina, the day is spent in prayer on the plains of **Arafat** until sunset. The night is spent in the region of **Muzadalifah**.
- The next day, Pilgrims 'stone the devil' at **Mina**. This is because it was here that Abraham had a vision of Satan and was ordered by the angel Gabriel to throw stones at him.
- In the following days, the Ka'aba in Mecca is again circled and, in Mina, the 'devil stoned' again. The Hajj is concluded by circling the Ka'aba again.

❓ Test Yourself

1 What are the major sites of pilgrimage for each major faith?

2 Why is Jerusalem so important to so many faiths?

⭐ Stretch Yourself

1 Why do people of faith go on pilgrimage?

Jewish and Christian Rites of Passage

Jewish Rites of Passage

1 Birth – Brit Milah

In Judaism, there are different birth ceremonies for boys and girls.

On the eighth day after birth, a **Mohel** (trained circumciser) will come to the boy's home and ritually remove his foreskin. During the ceremony of **Brit Milah**, the boy is circumcised and given his Hebrew name and his everyday name. The ceremony recalls God's **covenant** with Abraham and, traditionally, only men are present.

If the child is a girl, she will receive her name at the next public reading of the **Torah** in the synagogue.

2 Adolescence – Bar (Bat) Mitzvah

When boys are 13 and girls 12, they become **Bar/Bat Mitzvah** (son/daughter of the Law). The child is taught how to read the Hebrew Scriptures, tie their teffilin and wear the **Tallit**. On the next **Sabbath** after the appropriate birthday, the boy will be 'called up' to read from the Torah in the synagogue. His father will say a prayer and the boy will be blessed.

A similar ceremony is held for girls although she may not be 'called up' to read the Torah.

3 Marriage

Jewish weddings can be held on any day except the Sabbath or a major festival. They often take place in a synagogue. The bride and groom will fast before the marriage which will take place under the **Chuppah** (a canopy representing the marriage home). The service is usually conducted by a **rabbi** and begins with the signing of the **Ketubah** (contract).

During the ceremony, prayers will be said, glasses of wine drunk, scriptures read, rings exchanged, blessings given and a glass broken under foot. Traditionally, the groom wears black and the bride white. After the ceremony there is a reception.

4 Death

When a Jew dies, the body is prepared for burial, which must take place as soon as possible. It is never left unattended. The body is buried in a simple linen shroud, wrapped in a Tallit. This is often the Tallit that the Jewish person had been given for their Bar/Bat Mitzvah. A coffin is not necessary and the body must be in contact with the earth. Compromises are made to comply with local legal requirements, for example, in England, the coffin may have holes drilled in it so that contact with the earth may be maintained. Removal of organs and **cremation** are forbidden.

The ceremony usually takes place in the synagogue and will include the chanting of **psalms** and **eulogies** by family and friends. Following the funeral, there is a set period of **mourning**.

Christian Rites

1 Birth – Infant Baptism

Parents and **God-parents** bring the child to the priest who conducts the ceremony at the **font**. The priest asks them questions and they make **promises** about supporting the child in its Christian life. **Water** from the font is sprinkled on the baby's head and the sign of the **cross** made. He gives the baby its name and says: "I baptise you in the name of the Father, and of the Son, and of the Holy Spirit." A prayer may be said for the baby and the parents given a **lighted candle**.

Some denominations baptise adults and do so by total immersion (often known as '**Believer's Baptism'**). Some, including the Baptist Church, do not baptise infants. Some people who were baptised as babies choose to be totally immersed when they become Christians. It can also be important for those who wish to be confirmed but were not baptised as infants.

2 Adolescence – Confirmation

Confirmation is often referred to as '**the second part of baptism'**. Confirmation usually occurs when the child reaches adolescence but could be earlier.

After a period of training, the young person will present themselves to be confirmed. During the service, the Bishop will ask them to renew the promises made for them at baptism. They then make further promises and, as he **lays hands** on them, says '**receive the Holy Spirit'**. Prayers are said for them and then they will join the Bishop in saying the Apostles' Creed.

Once they have been confirmed, Holy Communion can be taken.

3 Marriage

Before getting married, a couple are usually expected to attend a **marriage preparation** course. During the ceremony, hymns will be sung, prayers said and scriptures read. The priest/vicar informs the congregation of the importance and meaning of marriage. The couple are invited to make their **promises** to each other: to love, comfort, honour and protect each other for the rest of their lives. They then make their vows before exchanging rings. The rings are **symbolic** of the eternal nature of marriage. After a sermon and blessing, the couple sign a legally-binding marriage certificate.

4 Death

Christian funerals usually take place about a **week** after a person dies. The service usually begins with the priest/vicar saying:

"**I am the resurrection and the life; he who believes in me shall live even if he dies.**"

(John 11:25)

During the service, hymns are sung and passages from the Bible are read. One favourite passage is **Psalm 23**. There is usually a short sermon and a friend or family member may speak about the person. The priest/vicar will then say a prayer that commends the person to God. After the service, there will be a burial or cremation.

❓ Test Yourself

❶ List the four rites of passage for Jews and Christians.

⭐ Stretch Yourself

❶ Trace the origins of circumcision and research the covenant with Abraham.

Muslim and Sikh Rites of Passage

Muslim Rites

1 Birth – Aqeeqah

Immediately after birth, the **Adhaan** (call to prayer) is whispered into the baby's ears by the father. A tiny part of a **date** is placed on the baby's lips. **Seven days** after birth, the baby's head is shaved, the hair weighed and the equivalent weight in gold or silver given to charity. The hair is then usually buried. The baby's name is given and boys are usually **circumcised** at this age, although it may be delayed. Sheep are slaughtered and the meat shared between family, friends and the poor. These birth rituals are called **Aqeeqah**. This is sometimes spelt **Aqiqah**.

2 Adolescence

Within Islam, there is no seperate ceremony for young people as they reach adolescence.

3 Marriage

Traditionally, Muslim marriages are arranged marriages and they vary greatly depending on the prevailing culture. There is a legal contract that protects the interests of the woman with a financial settlement from the husband (**mahr**).

The ceremony (known as **nikah**) is often a simple one with the Qur'an being read and a short sermon being preached by an Imam. Vows are exchanged before witnesses and a ring may be given. Most brides wear a white wedding dress but some brides favour the **shalwar-kameez** (scarlet with gold thread). It is common for them to have their hands and feet decorated with **henna**.

Following the ceremony there is usually a celebration.

4 Death – Funeral

If the death of a Muslim is expected, they (or someone else) will repeat the **call to prayer** so that it is the last thing that is heard. When a Muslim dies, **same gender** members of the family wash the body and wrap it in a simple white linen or cloth **shroud**. This takes place within hours of the death. Mourners then gather and say prayers of **forgiveness** for the dead.

As soon as possible, the body is buried in a grave, with the head facing Mecca. **Cremation** is forbidden. Further prayers are said and a three day period of **mourning** begins.

☿ Boost Your Memory

To help you remember the different rites of passage, draw a 'spider chart'.

Sikh Rites

1 Birth – Nam Karan

As soon after birth as reasonably possible, mother, baby and family attend worship in the gurdwara. Joyful hymns are recited from the Guru Granth Sahib. The family prepare **Karah Parshad** (sacred food) and present gifts to the Guru Granth Sahib. **Amrit** (sugar water) is given to the mother and the baby.

After the **Ardas** is said, the granthi opens the Guru Granth Sahib at random. The first letter on the page must be the first letter of the child's name. When the name is decided, it is announced to the congregation. If the baby is a boy, **Singh** (lion) is added to his name and **Kaur** (princess) if it is a girl.

2 Adolescence – Amrit

Sikh baptism can take place at any time and often after adolescence.

The ceremony is conducted in the presence of the Guru Granth Sahib by five 'loved ones', each wearing the five 'K's. (**Turbans** are always worn although they are not part of the five 'K's.) The principles of Sikhism are explained and are accepted. After the Ardas, the five stir the Amrit with their swords. Prayers are offered over the mixture, which is then sprinkled over the eyes and hair of the candidates. They sip the remaining Amrit. The **Mool Mantra** is repeated five times by all present. A passage from the Guru Granth Sahib is read and Karah Parshad is eaten.

If they break the Sikh laws, they must be re-baptised into the faith.

3 Marriage – Anand Karaj

Marriages can take place on any suitable day and are usually in the morning in the gurdwara. The couple sit in the presence of the Guru Granth Sahib, and hymns are sung. Traditionally, the man wears white and the woman red.

A baptised Sikh performs the marriage and begins by explaining the **duties** of married life. They bow before the book to show their acceptance of this.

The bridegroom wears a sash over his shoulder which is placed in the bride's hands. Verses are read from the Granth and the couple walk round the book, the groom leading the bride, to the singing of hymns. This is repeated four times.

After further readings from the Granth, Karah Parshad is eaten by all present. Following the ceremony there is a wedding banquet.

4 Death

After death, the body is prepared for the funeral with a **yoghurt** bath whilst prayers are said. The body is **dressed** in new clothes, including the five 'K's.

Before the cremation of the body, the Ardas is recited and prayers are said. Someone may say something about the person or a short talk may be given. A further service may also take place in the gurdwara.

After the cremation, the remains will be **scattered** on the surface of a river. Traditionally, the ashes would be scattered on the River Ganges.

? Test Yourself

1. How do Sikhs welcome babies into the faith?
2. How many days after birth is a Muslim's head shaved?

★ Stretch Yourself

1. What are the arguments for and against arranged marriages?
2. Why are death ceremonies so different in the above faiths?

Jewish and Christian Festivals

The Importance of Festivals

Festivals play a key role in the lives of believers. They mark **major points** in the life of the religion and usually have a foundation in **historical events**. They may be related to the birth, life or death of the founder or revered leader. Festivals may even relate to some specific season of the year. Whatever their reason, festivals are usually an opportunity for **collective celebration**.

Jewish Festivals

Jewish festivals are celebrated in the home at least as much as they are in the synagogue. There are numerous festivals, including:
- **Passover** – the escape from Egypt
- **Rosh Hashanah** – New Year
- **Yom Kippur** – the Day of Atonement

Passover (**Pesach**) is celebrated in the synagogue with special readings for each of the days throughout the week of Passover. However, the **Seder** meal at home is central. Before the day arrives, all **leaven** must be removed from the house and first-born males must fast.

How Jewish Festivals are Celebrated

The story of the **escape from Egypt** is told around the table through a series of questions and answers (**the Haggadah**). As the story unfolds, symbolic food is eaten from the Seder dish:
- **Matzo** – the unleavened bread at the escape
- **Lamb bone** – the paschal lamb sacrificed in the Temple
- **Roasted egg** – sacrifice and determination
- **Bitter herbs** – suffering in slavery
- **Lettuce**, etc. – new life
- **Salt water** – tears in slavery
- **Charoset** – sweet paste (apples, nuts, cinnamon and wine) representing the mortar slaves used to build Egyptian palaces
- **Four cups of wine** – liberty and joy
- **Elijah's cup** of wine – the promise of the Messiah

Passover is also called the **Festival of Freedom** and celebrates the importance of freedom for all people. Rosh Hashanah is the New Year festival and reminds Jews of the **creation** of the world. It is also a time of judgement which is concluded soon after at Yom Kippur.

In the synagogue, there are special services which culminate in the blowing of the **shofar** (ram's horn trumpet). In the home, there is a special meal which concentrates on **sweetness**. Apples are dipped in honey and sweet carrot stew is often served. **Pomegranates** feature because of the tradition that the fruit has **613 seeds** (613 laws). The sweetness symbolises the hope for a blessed New Year.

Just over a week after Rosh Hashanah comes Yom Kippur, the **Day of Atonement**. It is the most sacred of days and is understood to be the day when God makes the final decision on each person for the coming year. On this occasion, the synagogue is the focus. For Jews it is a time of **abstinence**. During the services, men wear their **prayer shawls** and the congregation confesses their sins. There are a series of five services which conclude with the final blowing of the shofar.

Christian Festivals

Advent and Christmas

Advent is the time of **preparation** for Christmas and begins on the Sunday closest to November 30. Advent **candles** are arranged in a **wreath** and a new candle is lit each Sunday. They each have religious significance. A **fifth** candle is lit on Christmas Day (the **birth** of Jesus).

Christmas celebrates the birth of Jesus (**Matthew 2/Luke 2**) and is a very joyful time for Christians. It is difficult to separate the religious symbolism about Christmas from the secular. Trees, cards, tinsel, turkey, Father Christmas, snow and so on are nothing to do with the birth of Jesus. However, lights, stars, gifts, the crib, nativity plays and carols are.

During the Christmas period, church worship is particularly bright and lively. Not only are Advent candles lit but Biblical readings focus on the birth of Jesus. **Carols** are special Christmas hymns that re-tell the stories about shepherds and angels, wise men and a star and the baby in a manger. Churches are specially decorated and there are often special services, such as **Midnight Mass** on Christmas Eve.

Lent

For forty days before Easter, Christians remember the forty days Jesus spent **fasting** and being tempted in the wilderness. For many Christians, Lent is marked by some type of fasting and, on **Ash Wednesday**, Christians are marked with a cross of ash on their forehead.

Shrove Tuesday is the day before the start of Lent and is a day of confession and forgiveness when Christians are '**shriven**'. Because Christians used to eat up all dairy products before the fast, Shrove Tuesday also became known as '**pancake day**'.

Easter

Although not as popular as Christmas, Easter is the most important festival in the Christian calendar. The festival lasts for a full week leading up to Easter Sunday.

- **Palm Sunday** – Jesus rode into Jerusalem on a donkey. Today, churches may hold **processions of witness** and **palm crosses** are often distributed.
- **Maundy Thursday** – Jesus and the disciples shared their **last supper** and he washed his disciples' feet. Special **Holy Communion** services are held and there are often **foot-washing** ceremonies.
- **Good Friday** – Jesus was **crucified** at Golgotha. This is the most solemn day of the Christian year. Churches are stripped of all colour and Christians spend time in quiet prayer and reflection as they '**keep a vigil at the cross**'. Readings and songs about the **Crucifixion** are common.
- **Easter Sunday** – Jesus was raised from the dead. Joyful and colourful worship celebrates the **resurrection** of Jesus. Christians greet each other with the words 'Christ is risen!' with the response 'He is risen indeed!'. The **paschal candle** may be lit and carried into the church to remind Christians that 'the Light of the World' has returned.

Pentecost

Pentecost is celebrated **fifty** days after Easter and recalls the coming of the **Holy Spirit** in power and the birth of the Christian Church. While **white** is the predominant colour that is worn, the **dove** and the **flame**, powerful symbols of the Holy Spirit, are much in evidence. Focus in worship is often on the '**gifts of the Spirit**'.

? Test Yourself

1 List the main events recalled in the Seder Meal and the foods that represent them.

2 How long does Lent last for?

★ Stretch Yourself

1 Explain why the various services during Easter vary so much in their nature and expression.

Muslim and Sikh Festivals

Muslim Festivals

Ramadan and Eid ul Fitr

Ramadan is the **ninth** month of the Muslim calendar and recalls the revelation of the **Qur'an** to the prophet Muhammad. It is sometimes called the '**month of the Qur'an**'. During Ramadan, all able Muslims must **fast** during daylight hours. The month begins with the sighting of the **new moon** and ends in the same way.

Each day's fast begins at **sunrise** and ends at **sunset**. Between these hours, no food or drink is to be taken although meals before sunrise and after sunset are consumed. Children, the old, infirm, pregnant women and the sick are exempt from the fast. Special prayers are said and the month is seen as an opportunity to increase self-control in all areas, including food, sleeping, sex and the use of time.

Following the month of Ramadan is the feast of Eid ul Fitr. Muslims thank Allah for the strength He has given them to complete the fast and celebrate the end of the month of fasting.

Festivities begin with the sighting of the new moon. Special services are held in the mosque and there are often processions out of doors. People buy new clothes, decorate their homes, buy each other gifts and send cards. There is a special Eid meal that is shared with family and friends, eaten, during daylight, for the first time in a month.

This is also seen as a time of forgiveness and making amends.

Eid ul Adha

In Muslim countries, this is a four-day festival that celebrates **Abraham's** (Ibrahim's) willingness to sacrifice his son in accordance with God's command. Emphasis is placed on each person's **submission** to Allah and their willingness to live sacrificial lives.

Muslims sacrifice a sheep which is distributed between family, friends and the poor. This is symbolic of Abraham's sacrifice. Presents are exchanged and there are special prayers.

Sikh Festivals

Diwali

Diwali is the **Festival of Lights** which celebrates the release from prison of the sixth guru, **Guru Hargobind** and 52 other princes in 1619. Sikhs celebrated his return by lighting the Golden Temple.

Traditionally, houses, shops and public places are decorated with rows of pottery lamps, fuelled by mustard oil. Oil lamps are floated on the **River Ganges**. Fireworks have become very popular and electric lights have become much more common.

Homes are decorated, **new clothes** bought, gifts given and special worship conducted in the gurdwara. It is also an opportunity to celebrate a successful **harvest**.

Baisakhi

The **New Year** festival celebrates the creation of the **Khalsa** by Guru Gobind Singh in 1699. Five men who volunteered to sacrifice their lives for their faith were sprinkled with **Amrit** and became the basis for the Sikh brotherhood. It is a very popular day for Sikhs to be **baptised** into the Sikh brotherhood.

Traditionally, the **Nishan Sahib** (Sikh flag) is replaced with a new one. When the flag is removed, the flag pole is cleaned and washed and a new flag replaced. The ceremony is completed with an **Ardas**.

There are parades, dancing, singing and chanting of scripture, and talks are given about the importance of the festival.

✓ Maximise Your Marks

If you can recall the events when Guru Gobind Singh established the Khalsa and explain why Baisakhi is so important for Sikhs you will gain higher marks.

❓ Test Yourself

1. List each of the main festivals mentioned above.
   a) Briefly describe each.
   b) Describe the origin of each.
   c) Explain how each is celebrated.

⭐ Stretch Yourself

1. What are festivals and why are they important for believers?

Jewish and Christian Views on Afterlife

Is There Life After Death?

This is one of the most fundamental questions that anyone can ask. Unfortunately, the answer is not as easy as the question. There is plenty of **evidence** to help with the debate: many people claim to have had **Near Death Experiences**, others to be able to communicate with the dead and still others who claim to have seen **ghosts**. However, there is no clear scientific **proof**.

Each of the world's religions has addressed this issue but, in the end, it is a matter of faith. The two main areas of belief involve either the existence of **heaven and hell**, or the existence of **reincarnation**.

Judaism

There is a wide spectrum of beliefs about the afterlife in Judaism. There has always been a clear focus on the here and now in Judaism and, therefore, little clear teaching about the afterlife. Consequently, it is quite possible for an Orthodox Jew to believe that the souls of the **righteous dead** go to **heaven**. It is also possible to believe that they will remain in limbo until the **Messiah** comes to **resurrect** them. Wicked souls could be destroyed at death or spend eternity being tormented by demons.

The **Torah** clearly emphasises the here and now and there is little support for the overt belief in heaven or hell. In the time of Jesus there was a definite division between the **Pharisees** and **Sadducees** over the issue. The Sadducees found no basis for belief in it in scripture, whilst the Pharisees sited various passages that could be understood to support it.

Other Jewish Beliefs

Contemporary belief embraces both the idea of a spiritual heaven and hell, whilst also allowing for the impending 'Messianic Age'. Refusal to allow the **cremation** of the dead is an indication of these widely held beliefs.

Christianity

Jesus taught that He was the 'resurrection and the life' and that all 'who believe in me will live, even though they die'. (John 11, verse 25ff). In John 3, verse 16, we read that, 'God so loved the world that he gave his one and only Son, that whoever believes in him shall not perish but have eternal life'. Christians believe that, three days after his crucifixion, God raised Jesus back to life (**resurrection**). This life after death is a central Christian belief. All who accept Jesus as Lord and Saviour have the hope of this resurrection life.

However, Christians also believe in **justice** and **judgement** and that the wicked will be punished. After death, God will **judge** all in accordance with how they have lived their lives on Earth.

Although heaven and hell are mentioned in the Bible, there is little by way of clear description. Some Christians think of heaven and hell as physical '**places**' where they go after death. Others see them as **states of being** where their soul lives on.

Heaven is understood to be a blessed existence, united with God. **Eternity** is spent in His presence in the company of all those others who have been 'saved'. It is a joyful existence and is fervently to be hoped for. **Hell**, on the other hand, is the opposite. It is seen as being where souls are **separated** from God for ever. Whether they are '**punished**' is unclear but this separation is to be avoided at all costs.

Other Christian Beliefs

There is a debate about whether believers from other faiths can attain heaven. Some Christians hold that only those who have been committed to Jesus will be present. Others believe that those who have not had the opportunity to respond to Jesus will be judged by the good they have done in the light of the truth that they knew.

Many Roman Catholics believe in **Purgatory**. This is an in-between state of cleansing and preparation for heaven for those who are not automatically received into heaven or condemned to hell.

Christians also believe that Jesus will return again from heaven to Earth. This will not be the same as His first coming but will bring in the resurrection of the dead and the final judgement. This is known as the Second Coming or the **Parousia**.

Religious Practice

✓ Maximise Your Marks

Knowing the meaning of the following terms and being able to define them accurately will gain higher marks:
- Resurrection
- Eternity
- Purgatory
- Parousia
- Judgement

❓ Test Yourself

1. If Jews believe in heaven, how can they attain it?

2. List three images that you would associate with the Christian concept of heaven and three for hell.

⭐ Stretch Yourself

1. Not all Christians believe in Purgatory. Why is it important for Catholics?

Muslim and Sikh Views on Afterlife

Islam

Muslims believe that Allah is in control of all things. However, He has given mankind **free will** and, consequently, people have the choice to do right or wrong. Because there will be a **day of judgement**, they are responsible for their own actions. They have one life and they must live it accordingly.

When the **Day of Resurrection** comes, all people will have their good deeds weighed against their bad deeds by Allah Himself. Until the day arrives, the dead will remain in their graves. If the balance is in their favour, they will go to **Paradise** where they will enjoy an eternity of bliss and blessing. However, if the bad outweighs the good, they will be punished in **hell**. Not only are deeds and actions taken into account, Allah also weighs a person's intentions.

For many Muslims, Paradise ('the Garden' – **Janna**) is a place of physical and spiritual pleasure. There are wonderful mansions, delicious food and drink and virgin companions. It is a place of reward and blessing. On the other hand, hell (**Jahannam**) is a place of physical and spiritual suffering. There are seven levels of this fiery crater, the lowest of which contains a cauldron of burning pitch. One's level in hell is dependent on the severity of offences committed.

Muslims believe that Allah is **merciful** and forgiving and some believe that even people who have lived bad lives can enter Paradise if they are truly **repentant** and have been punished. Because He is merciful and compassionate, some Muslims believe that hell will eventually be empty. However, others believe that not everything can be forgiven. They believe that refusal to worship Allah can never be forgiven.

Other Muslim Beliefs

There is an interesting debate in Islam about the destination of **suicide bombers**. Some believe that Paradise awaits those who lose their lives in Jihad (holy war). So, those who blow themselves up to take the lives of the enemy will be rewarded.

However, others point out that suicide and the killing of others is forbidden in Islam and, consequently, they will go to hell. The debate amongst Muslims continues, unresolved.

Sikhism

Sikhs believe that human life is the last stage in the soul's progress towards becoming one with God. The ultimate aim is to eventually end the **cycle of birth, life, death and rebirth** and the **transmigration** of the soul. Although the body dies, the soul is immortal and, at death, moves on to the next stage of existence. The soul of the good person will find favour in the next life but the soul of the evil person will continue in the unending cycle of birth and death. This will produce existence in a lower form and take this soul further away from union with God. **Guru Nanak** said, 'According to one's actions, one gets near to or distant from God'. The best action for the individual in this life is to **meditate** on the name and nature of God.

This assessment and redirection of the soul is known as **Karma**: a person is rewarded or punished according to their actions. For Sikhs, there is clear **judgement**. This judgement is true and honest and no spiritual leader can sway this judgement. Although Karma is inexorable, repentance, prayer and love can earn God's grace which can neutralise a person's previous Karma. True repentance and dedication to God invokes God's mercy and hastens the longed for union.

'Mukti' is the term used for this concept of the **emancipation** (setting free) of the soul from the cycle of **reincarnation**. 'Mukti' has a negative and a positive aspect. Negatively, it is to do with the release from bondage to ignorance, suffering, passion, desire, superstition, the wheel of life and so on. These attachments are perilous for the existence of the soul. On the positive side, it signifies the realisation of the true self: a self, freed from the cares of the here and now, existing in the everlasting peace of the eternal and infinite. It is the escape from bondage: liberation.

Other Sikh Beliefs

The Sikh attitude to **heaven and hell** is an interesting one. Although the concept of heaven and hell exists in Sikhism, it is generally believed to be symbolic. The imagery of oceans of fire and flame, poisonous flames and terrible tortures is considered to be more a state of mind of the person living outside the presence of God. Similarly the bliss experienced in 'heaven' is the joy of living in the presence of God.

The true Sikh is neither afraid of hell nor anxious for a place in heaven: they are both conditions of the mind. Heaven and hell are not '**places**', external from the individual. They are states of mind in which they live. Some Sikhs hold that living in prosperity in this life is heaven and that being a beggar on the streets is hell. However, others point out that a rich and successful person can be in torment (hell) and a beggar can be close to God (heaven). For most, the concept of heaven and hell is an illustration of the doctrine of Karma and not actual places. Guru Arjan said, 'Wherever the praises of God are sung, there is heaven'.

? Test Yourself

1. Describe what each of the above faiths teach about:
   a) Heaven and hell and
   b) Salvation

2. What does 'judgement' mean in each of these faiths?

★ Stretch Yourself

1. What is reincarnation and how can Sikhs escape it?

Practice Questions

Complete these exam-style questions to test your understanding. Check your answers on page 91. You may wish to answer these questions on a separate piece of paper.

1 Describe why a religious believer may choose to go on a pilgrimage. (5)

2 Describe how one religion uses its holy book during worship. (4)

3 Describe the purpose and value of prayer for a religious believer. (4)

4 Explain the purpose of birth rite in one religion. (5)

5 Explain the effects that pilgrimage might have on a religious believer. (5)

6 Explain why festivals are important in religion. (4)

....

....

....

....

7 For all of the following questions, explain whether you agree with the statement. You must then give reasons to support your answer and show that you have thought about different points of view. You must refer to the teachings of at least one religion in your answer.

a) "I don't need to go to my holy building to worship God because He is everywhere." (4)

....

....

....

....

b) "People should spend their money helping others rather than using it to go on a pilgrimage." (4)

....

....

....

....

c) "I know that if I try and do the right thing in life then I will be with God when I die." (4)

....

....

....

....

....

How well did you do?

0–24	Try again	25–29	Getting there	30–34	Good work	35–39	Excellent!

Origins of Crime and Punishment

Sins and Crimes

Many of the laws that govern the UK have their origin in the **10 commandments**. They are found in the Bible and the Torah in **Exodus 20, verses 1–17**, and were given by God to Moses on Mount Sinai.

In religious terms, all of us commit sins but only a few commit crimes. A sin is when actions or thoughts contradict the teachings of a religion, therefore making it an act against God. For example, adultery is clearly a sin for Jews and Christians as it is against the seventh Commandment, yet it is not a crime under UK law. Crimes are actions against the laws of the country or state. However, crimes are almost always sins as well.

The list below shows a shortened version of each commandment.

1. You shall have no other gods before me.
2. You shall not make for yourself an idol.
3. Do not take the name of the Lord in vain.
4. Remember the Sabbath and keep it holy.
5. Honour your father and mother.
6. You shall not kill/murder.
7. You shall not commit adultery.
8. You shall not steal.
9. You shall not bear false witness against your neighbour.
10. You shall not covet anything that belongs to your neighbour.

Jesus' Teachings

During His life, Jesus was faced with many questions about sins and crimes and what the punishments for them should be. Whether He was faced with Pharisees asking about taxes, a mob wanting to stone an adulteress woman or trading in the temple, Jesus always had a response that focused on what He taught were the two greatest commandments.

Jesus said unto him, "You shall love the Lord your God with all your heart, and with all your soul, and with all your mind. This is the first and great commandment. And the second is like unto it, you shall love your neighbour as thyself."
(Matthew 22, verses 37–39)

By these commandments, Jesus was teaching that all actions should be out of love for another person. Christians call this the Golden Rule.

When asked about taxes in Matthew 22, verses 15–22, Jesus knew the crowd were trying to trick Him. The Pharisees asked Jesus whether they should pay taxes or not to the Romans. They hoped that Jesus would say no because the Jews did not like the ruling Roman laws. If Jesus had said this then He would have been committing a crime and therefore sinning. Instead, in verses 17–21, Jesus replied:

"You hypocrites, why are you trying to trap me? Show me the coin used for paying the tax." They brought him a denarius, and he asked them, "Whose portrait is this? And whose inscription?" "Caesar's," they replied. Then he said to them, "Give to Caesar what is Caesar's, and to God what is God's."

This shows that Jesus stated that paying tax to Caesar was right as he (Caesar) ran the country.

The Pharisees were always keen to try and catch Jesus out and for Him to condone or allow something that went against some of His other teachings. In John 7, verses 53–8:11 Jesus is confronted by a crowd who have caught a woman in the act of adultery. Under the law she should have been stoned to death for her actions. When Jesus is asked what should be done He simply answers: **"He who is without sin should cast the first stone"**.

Jesus' Teachings (cont.)

By this, Jesus is saving the woman from being stoned without condoning the act of adultery.

The account of Jesus overturning the tables appears in all four Gospels, for example Mark 11, verses 15–19. This suggests it is of great importance. In these passages, Jesus challenges the sellers and traders who have their stalls inside the city temple. Scripture teaches that this should be a sacred space and they are abusing it. Using **righteous anger**, Jesus states that they had turned the temple into a '**den of thieves**'. With this He overturned the tables and ordered them out of the temple. This shows that Jesus stood up for what He believed in and wanted to see justice for the sins that were being committed.

Aims of Punishment

Each type of punishment aim serves a different purpose and is influenced by the crime committed.

- **Deterrence** – where the punishment for a crime is so severe it aims to stop people from committing the crime in the first place, for example, the death penalty for murder.
- **Rehabilitation** – the punishment tries to help the criminal to not commit the crime again by changing their behaviour and point of view.
- **Restoration** – the victims of the crime are seen as being of most importance and the punishment given to the criminal may bring closure for them.
- **Retribution** – this sees the criminal pay for the crime that they have committed. It should help the victim to see the criminal punished – the problem is working out what the punishment will be.

💡 Boost Your Memory

To help you remember, draw a simple set of scales. Briefly list the strengths and weaknesses of each aim of punishment. Which appears to be the strongest of the four?

The Effects of Crime

Crime directly affects the victims of the crime, but often extends beyond these people to others. In some cases, the victim loses their life or possessions or maybe suffers physical or psychological harm. Beyond that the families of victims have to endure the pain that their loved ones have gone through and they may be required to support them physically due to injuries or loss of possessions.

Wider Effects of Crime

The effects of crime can be very far reaching. Society in general often suffers because of crime. People may get frightened when they hear about crimes through the media. Insurance premiums may go up and council tax can go up to pay for extra security and/or lighting.

❓ Test Yourself

1. What is the difference between a sin and a crime?
2. How does the aim of deterrence work?

⭐ Stretch Yourself

1. Why might the 10 Commandments be viewed as being an out-of-date set of rules?

Religious Attitudes

Views on Crime and Punishment

The Death Penalty

The question as to whether or not it is morally acceptable for people to be executed, and if so under what circumstances, has been debated for centuries. The problems involved include the general moral issues of punishment and then whether it is ever morally right to end a life. In the UK, the last executions were Peter Anthony Allen at Liverpool and Gwynne Owen Evans at Manchester Prisons. Both were hanged on 13 August 1964. Since then any executions have taken place outside of the UK. However, some UK citizens have been executed in other countries. China has the highest record for the use of the death penalty.

Islamic Views on Crime and Law

Islamic countries that practise a very strict Sharia law are associated with the use of capital punishment as retribution for the largest variety of crimes. At the other end of the spectrum are countries such as Albania and Bosnia, which still retain the death penalty as part of their penal system, but are abolitionist in practice:

"Take not life, which God has made sacred, except by way of justice and law. Thus does He command you, so that you may learn wisdom." (Qur'an 6:151)

In Islamic law, the death penalty is appropriate for two types of crime:
- Intentional murder: In these cases the victim's family is given the option as to whether or not to insist on a punishment of this severity.

- Fasadfil-ardh ('spreading mischief in the land'): Islam permits the death penalty for anyone who threatens to undermine authority or destabilise the state.

'Spreading mischief in the land' is open to interpretation, but the following crimes are usually included:
- treason/apostasy (when one leaves the faith and turns against it)
- terrorism
- piracy of any kind
- rape
- adultery
- homosexual activity

Christian Views on Crime and Law

For Christians, teaching in the New Testament is very different to that in the Old Testament.

"Eye for an eye, tooth for a tooth. As he has injured the others so he is to be injured." (Leviticus 24, verses 19–20)

This passage would suggest that if you took somebody's life then you should lose your own.

This argument was supported by **St Augustine** in his book **The City of God**, where he wrote:

"The same divine law which forbids the killing of a human being allows certain exceptions, as when God authorises killing by a general law or when He gives an explicit commission to an individual for a limited time."

Some Jews still follow this teaching but for Christians the teaching in the New Testament and of the Church shows that it is wrong.

"For rulers hold no terror for those who do right, but for those who do wrong." (Romans 13:3)

In his writing, Paul is saying that those in charge must not do so with fear over their people. The death penalty would clearly bring fear. The Catholic Church has generally remained in favour of capital punishment in those cases where the crime committed was suitably extreme. However, by the end of this century opinions were changing. In 1980, the **National Conference of Catholic Bishops** published an almost entirely negative statement on capital punishment.

> ## Boost Your Memory
>
> To help you remember the key aspects of war, write down the word WAR and create two mnemonics, one showing the three key strengths of war and the other the three key weaknesses.

Relative Punishments

Should every crime require a punishment? The obvious answer is of course yes, but there are times when the consequences of crime may need to be carefully adjusted.

In some cases, it could be argued that an individual has no alternative but to commit a crime. Some may steal food to feed their family, a wife may kill her husband following a prolonged period of abuse.

In these cases, courts often take circumstances into consideration when deciding what punishments should be given. Lesser sentences, suspended sentences and on occasion no punishments may be given, due to the position that the 'criminal' found themselves in.

> ## ✓ Maximise Your Marks
>
> Showing that you understand the impact that the death penalty can have both in a positive and negative way will gain higher marks.

> ## ❓ Test Yourself
>
> ❶ Pick three circumstances under which a Muslim would allow the death penalty.
>
> ❷ Think of a suitable crime for each aim of punishment and explain your answer.
>
> ❸ What do you think is the best way to reduce crime?

> ## ⭐ Stretch Yourself
>
> ❶ Explain your view on the use of the death penalty, including views different to your own.

Forgiveness

Forgive and Forget

For a religious believer, true forgiveness requires a commitment to not act wrongly again and a decision to change the way in which they behave.

They may also have to perform an act of **penance**, showing that they are truly sorry for their actions before God.

Forgiveness in Christianity

The topic of forgiveness is arguably one of the key foundations to Christianity. When a baby is introduced to the faith through **Baptism**, the ceremony sees the sins that the child has been born with being washed away and forgiven.

Jesus' last words before dying on the cross are recorded as being, **'Father forgive them, for they know not what they do'** (Luke 23, verse 34) Many Christians use this as the ultimate example of forgiveness, but there are many examples about it in the New Testament.

During His teaching, Jesus stated that the laws of the Old Testament were being replaced.

"You have heard it said 'Eye for an eye, tooth for a tooth', but I tell you. Do not resist an evil person. If someone strikes you on the right cheek, turn and offer him the left." (Matthew 5, verses 38–39)

Jesus wanted people to see that forgiveness should be given freely and can often bring a swift resolution to a difficult situation. Christians also acknowledge that without forgiveness, they can never enter into heaven.

"We have all sinned, and if we want to be forgiven by God, we must forgive others. If you do not forgive men their sins, your Father will not forgive your sins." (Matthew 6, verse 15)

In addition to this, Christians are also taught that only God is the true judge and that humans can only ever judge by earthly standards.

"Do not judge, or you too will be judged." (Matthew 7, verse 1)

This teaching from the Sermon on the Mount shows that it is dangerous to view the acts of others and judge them. Instead Christians should follow this teaching to ensure their salvation:

"If we confess our sins, he [God] is faithful and just and will forgive us our sins and purify us from all unrighteousness." (1 John 1, verse 9)

Forgiveness in Judaism

The history of Judaism has seen much suffering, including many battles found in the Tenakh and of course the atrocities of the holocaust. Jewish text teaches that to save a single life is to save an entire world. This therefore also means that the suffering of one is shared by the world. In Judaism, forgiveness of the individual cannot be separated from how it affects the community. For a Jew to reach **shleimut,** he/she must be willing to forgive those both inside and outside of their community.

Forgiveness enables a victim to put a hurtful incident behind them, restore a meaningful and compatible relationship and allow the wrongdoer the opportunity to reconcile. This concept of healing and repair is central to Judaism, as Jews are taught to practice **TikkunOlam**, the repairing of the world.

Forgiveness in Islam

Muslims place great value in the forgiveness Allah hands out but know they have to forgive others too. They do not expect Allah's forgiveness unless they also forgive those who do wrong to them, which includes their enemies. In the Qur'an Allah has described the Believers as:

"... those who avoid major sins and acts of indecencies and when they are angry they forgive." (al-Shura 42, verse 37)

In the same passage Allah teaches that the reward for evil is evil but the reward for forgiveness is given by Allah in the afterlife. Later in the Qur'an Muslims are taught that:

"If you punish, then punish with the like of that wherewith you were afflicted. But if you endure patiently, indeed it is better for the patient. Endure you patiently. Your patience is not except through the help of Allah." (al-Nahl 16, verses 126–127)

Again, this is teaching that forgiveness in this life leads to blessings after it.

Forgiveness in Sikhism

Sikhs also see the value of forgiveness. They believe that all forgives is given from God and helps them to overcome the suffering of this world. It is the responsibility of every Sikh to follow the example that their God has set for them.

"There is no other like the Merciful God. He is contained deep within each and everyone. He embellishes His devotees here and hereafter. God, It is Your nature to purify the sinners." (Guru Granth Sahib Ji, 866)

This raises interesting questions about earthly punishments for crimes. Although the criminal may be forgiven for their acts, they still need to face the consequences of their crimes according to the law of the land.

✓ Maximise Your Marks

If you can compare your views on what forgiveness is with that of a religion you will gain higher marks. In your view, which would create a better society if universally applied?

❓ Test Yourself

1. What is forgiveness?
2. When might forgiving someone be difficult?
3. Why is it in the interests of a religious believer to forgive others?
4. How could forgiveness lead to more forgiveness?

⭐ Stretch Yourself

1. If you have been forgiven, does this mean that you don't have to face consequences? Why?
2. Explain how the teaching of the Old Testament on forgiveness is very different to that in the New Testament.

Stewardship

Taking Care of The Planet

Humans largely control how the planet is looked after. However, many would argue that throughout history they have not done very well. The vast majority of religious believers feel that it is their responsibility to look after the planet as they believe that their God has trusted them with it. For Christians and Jews, **Genesis 1**, **verse 28**, tells them to subdue the Earth. This is often interpreted as meaning that they should ensure that they do not damage the environment and the Earth can be passed on to the next generation. Recent studies would suggest that although half of the world are religious believers, they have not done a great job in protecting the world.

For Muslims, **Khalifah** explains how they should treat the planet and respond to the damage that has already been done to it. Like Christians, they believe that their God, Allah, has created the world and has trusted humans to care for it.

💡 Boost Your Memory

Using www.biblegateway.com, find two more quotes instructing Christians how to look after the planet.

Damage to the Planet

The practice of **deforestation** has seen huge areas of land across the world stripped of trees for mainly housing or farming. This is most common in the Amazon rainforest, Brazil, where hundreds of thousands of acres of land have been cut down in just the last years. This not only destroys habitat but also reduces the amount of oxygen being released into the atmosphere. Many Christians try and support **maintained sustainable forests**, mainly found in Europe, as these replace the trees that are cut down. Big companies like **Kleenex**, state that they will plant more trees than they use for their products.

Air, **water** and **soil** pollution are common across the world. Use of fossil fuels (coal, oil, petrol and gas) not only cause pollution when extracted but when there are accidental spillages, for example, the BP oil pipe break in the USA in 2010. However, they cause a much greater level of atmospheric pollution when they are burnt.

💡 Boost Your Memory

To help you remember key concepts relating to stewardship, use the Internet to research two case studies where human actions have caused damage to the Earth. For each study, note where the damage has happened; how it has affected local animals and humans; and how it could have been prevented.

The Importance of Recycling

One of the best ways for a religious believer to help protect the world is to make changes in their own life. In 2009, the UK Government launched a programme focusing on three R's:

- **Reduce** – use less whenever possible
- **Reuse** – find another use for an item
- **Recycle** – when an item is beyond use and turned into something else

This was endorsed by Christians, Muslims, Sikhs and Jews as its aims are to conserve the Earth's resources.

A Religious Believer's Response

Although some would argue that it would not make a huge difference to the world, there are a number of actions that a religious believer could take. These actions include the following:

- Vote for political parties with an environmental policy.
- Pray to their God or gods to help with the problems the world is facing.
- Make an effort to use less fuel at home.
- Reduce the amount that they use their cars to save petrol.
- Join peaceful protests to raise awareness about environmental issues.

✓ Maximise Your Marks

Research the work of environmental organisations that a religious believer could join, e.g., TearFund.

❓ Test Yourself

1. What does Stewardship mean?
2. List three ways in which a religious believer could help solve damage done to the Earth.
3. Suggest things that the UK government could do to reduce its carbon footprint.
4. Explain the idea behind the '3 R's'.

⭐ Stretch Yourself

1. Compare and contrast the teachings on the environment from the Bible and the Qur'an.
2. Describe what *sustainability* means.

Relationships and the Family

The Family

For many people, their family is the people who they live with. Often this is made up of their parents and their siblings. In some cases, it may be added to by the presence of other relatives such as grandparents.

A Religious Family

In many respects, the religious family is very similar to a secular one. Both are often built around a married couple. The majority of religious families are based on a heterosexual relationship with the proportion being based on a homosexual relationship being greater in a secular family. A religious family may spend more planned time together as they are likely to worship and read scriptures together, for example, Jews celebrate **Shabbat** together, with each member of the family having roles to play in the ceremony. There are also rules for Christians to follow in the family. For example, the fifth Commandment in Exodus 20 reads:

"Honour father and mother."

Why do People get Married?

Although the numbers of people getting married has fallen in recent years, thousands of people still **tie the knot** every year in the UK. The primary reason for this is that the couple are in **love** with each other and want to commit themselves to this through marriage. Marriage is a legal contract and binds the couple together in the eyes of the law. For many religious believers, marriage gives them the opportunity to promise their lives to each other in the eyes of their God or gods, inside a holy building. It also allows them the opportunity to try and have children, as they believe that sex should only take place inside a marriage.

"Offer them [women] your wealth and the protection of wedlock rather than using them for the unfettered satisfaction of lust." (Surah 4)

✓ Maximise Your Marks

Ensure you understand why marriage is important in religion – ensure that you know two quotes from scripture to show this.

Marriage in Religions

Each religion has a different way of celebrating the marriage ceremony but all seek to highlight the importance of the union in the eyes of the law before God. They also place great value on the promises that the couple make to each other, for example in the Christian ceremony, promising to stay married until death. Christians believe that God has always planned for man and woman to be joined in marriage, from the moment that He created Adam and Eve.

"In the beginning God created them Male and Female. For this reason a man shall leave his father and mother and be joined to his wife, and the two shall become one flesh." (Mark 10, verse 7)

Jews, Muslims and Sikhs also place great value on the union of marriage. Each religion views the union as promises before their God. They all also believe that the family is the heart of society and proves the best environment for personal faith to grow in, with parents teaching their children about their religion. Through this, the faiths in general are likely to grow as the family spends time with their friends and through bringing people into their home.

Divorce

In today's UK society, many marriages still end in divorce, although this number is falling. In 2008, the divorce rate in England and Wales fell to 11.2 divorcing people per 1000 married population compared with the 2007 figure of 11.8, a fall of 5.1 per cent, the lowest level since 1979. Christians have different views about divorce and remarriage. The Protestant Church accepts divorce and believe that remarriage of divorcees is possible if a priest is confident of the couple's commitment to marriage. The Catholic Church teaches that divorce is not possible although an

annulment (when the marriage is declared 'not to have happened') is sometimes granted. Therefore, remarriage is not possible.

Muslims accept that divorce is possible, but the couple must have tried to stay together three times first. Therefore, a Muslim can remarry. Sikhs believe that marriage is a sacred union and must be maintained at all costs. There are rare occasions where it may be allowed, but this must be with the blessing of their gurdwara. This of course makes remarriage rare as well.

Religious Attitudes

? Test Yourself

1 List two reasons why someone might choose to get married.

2 State two ways in which a religious family may be different to a secular one.

3 Give two reasons why divorce rates in the UK might be falling.

4 Why might marriage be the best place to have children?

⭐ Stretch Yourself

1 'Remarriage is not as important as marriage.' Explain the arguments for and against this statement.

Poverty and Wealth

Religious Attitudes

Different Degrees of Poverty

Dependent upon location, what is deemed as being in poverty can differ greatly because of circumstances. Someone in the UK living in poverty may well have a roof over their heads and have clothes in their wardrobes but may have to make decisions as to how they divide their money between heating bills and buying food.

Another person living in Sierra Leone may be living in poverty and will have only the clothes that they stand in, no home and will not know where their next meal is coming from. Both are living in poverty but clearly there is a significant margin between them. Poverty is relative to the place in which people live.

Causes of Poverty

There are many causes of poverty, some of which are caused by humans and others which are not. The divide between the poverty of the third world and the wealth of the Western world can be attributed to human greed and exploitation. Throughout history much of Africa has seen its resources used by and sold by richer countries and the money taken from Africa. In later years some of these countries have then borrowed millions of pounds to buy weapons that they may not have needed and ended up with debts that they can't even afford the interest on.

Other countries, such as Haiti, have seen their homes and buildings destroyed by earthquakes and other natural disasters, forcing people into poverty as they don't have the funds to rebuild them.

✓ Maximise Your Marks

In the weeks before your exam, make sure you spend time watching the news. Print off images of poverty that you see from around the world. Annotate these to show the causes and possible solutions to these situations. Then, note how one religion may view the problem.

How can Poverty be Eased?

Every religion teaches its followers to help those around them, and this includes the poor. Many believers will support the work of charities, such as **Traidcraft, Christian Aid** etc., as a way of indirectly helping. For **Muslims**, helping the poor is one of the **Five Pillars** that they must follow, Zakat. As well as giving money, a Muslim will also fast during the month of Ramadan to help them sympathise with the poor and their needs.

Much of the world's poverty is caused by debt. Jews and Christians have specific teachings that they can follow to overcome this.

"At the end of every seven years ... every creditor shall release what he has lent to his neighbour ..." (i.e. cancel any debts) (Deuteronomy 15, verses 7–8)

This shows that those in debt should not have it held over them, forcing them into poverty, and should instead be given the opportunity to be freed from their debts. A religious believer could also ensure that they only purchase **fair trade** goods to ensure that the poorest people receive as much money for their products as possible.

Is it Wrong for a Religious Believer to be Rich?

If a religious believer should always help those who have less than them, it could be argued that it would be wrong for a believer to be rich. Christians are taught that money should never be their sole focus in life.

"For the love of money is the root of all evil: which while some coveted after, they have erred from the faith, and pierced themselves through with many sorrows." (Timothy 6, verse 10)

This does not say that money is the root of all evil but the love of it is, as this would make a person greedy and selfish. Jesus also taught that Christians should think about the afterlife when they think about possessions and money.

"Do not store up riches for yourself here on earth. Instead store up riches in heaven." (Matthew 6, verse 19)

Religious Attitudes

✔ Maximise Your Marks

Showing that you understand how being rich can bring about both positive and negative consequences for a religious believer will gain higher marks.

❓ Test Yourself

1. State two ways in which poverty can be different depending upon which country the person lives in.

2. List two ways in which poverty could be eased.

3. Why might being rich be a problem for a religious believer?

4. How might someone get into debt?

⭐ Stretch Yourself

1. In Matthew 19, Jesus teaches that it is harder for a rich man to enter heaven than it is for a camel to enter through the eye of a needle. What do you think this means?

2. Does money bring about more good than bad?

Theodicy

Does God Care?

How can an all-loving God exist when we see so much suffering around us every day? It would be hard to deny that there isn't suffering being experienced all of the time, somewhere in the world. However, is this evil caused by humans, or is it part of the natural world?

Christian and Jewish Theodicy

Theodicy, the problem of evil, is often used to try and show that there is no god in existence. One of the most famous examples of how theodicy can be used to show that God does not exist was written by Epicurus. He wrote:

1. If an all-powerful and perfectly good God exists, then evil does not.
2. There is evil in the world.
3. Therefore, an all-powerful and perfectly good God does not exist.

The logic of Epicurus' thoughts is very straight forward but still leaves a question of people. The primary Christian and Jewish response to this is based on the account of Adam and Eve. In **Genesis 2**, Adam and Eve live in the perfection of the Garden of Eden but are tempted to eat fruit from the Tree of Knowledge. As this is against the will of God, they sin. This is the first recorded sin in the Bible. Christians argue that this shows that man was given **free will** by God, an ability to choose what decisions they make. As Adam and Eve made the wrong decision, and therefore sinned, this passage has become known as **the fall of man** (when humanity was separated from God by their actions).

This separation meant that man had brought suffering upon himself. God sent both Adam and Eve from the garden, burdened Eve with pain during childbirth and Adam with the difficulty of farming barren land. From this, Christians and Jews argue that God did not cause the suffering but allowed the consequences of their actions to unfold. This view continues to the present day, with the simple belief being that God does not cause the suffering that we see, but because of our 'free will', we cause the situations ourselves and God allows us to experience the consequences of these actions.

The book of **Job** in the Old Testament, accounts Satan challenging God over the faithfulness of a man called Job. Job worships God but Satan states that this is only because Job is blessed by God. God allows Satan to **test** Job and throughout the book Satan fills Job's life with despair and tragedy. However, despite this, Job continues to worship God, who then restores Job's life to fullness. Jews and Christians both argue that this shows that God is not the cause of suffering but is able to remove it when it is part of His **sovereign plan**.

Islamic and Sikh Theodicy

In Islam, everything that is good in the world has been made or caused by Allah. A Muslim believes that life on Earth is a test, so that suffering in life is rewarded in the afterlife. Therefore, anyone who does not follow the will of Allah will face negative consequences when their life ends.

This view is very similar to the Christian view and Muslims also believe in the principle of free will. They argue that Allah has allowed intelligence and wisdom to understand what is bad and good in every situation. If Allah were to intervene in life on Earth then it would undermine the 'free will' that He has given. Instead, Muslims believe that bad deeds lead people to learn not to repeat mistakes. Allah allows people to make mistakes so that they can learn the right way and follow His teachings.

Sikhs believe that humans suffer in this life for one of two key reasons:
1. People either deny the existence of God, or
2. People are selfish in their actions, not thinking of others.

This can be overcome by human effort, self-reflection, and divine grace (**Gurprasad**) through the Guru's teachings. Sikhs believe that evil itself or any demonic life forms do not exist. Instead they believe that only failings of the human spirit or conscience lead to actions that cause suffering to others.

For a Sikh, the denial of the existence of God means that they are unable to call on him for help and support. When acting selfishly, the individual is acting outside of the will of God and puts themselves in situations where God does not want them to be.

⚡ Boost Your Memory

To help you remember the strengths and weaknesses of the belief that theodicy shows that there is no god, draw a table or a spider diagram.

❓ Test Yourself

1 Explain what theodicy is.

2 Describe what suffering is.

3 How can man help overcome suffering in the world?

4 Why does the problem of evil suggest that there is no god?

★ Stretch Yourself

1 If you were a god would you allow suffering? Explain your view.

2 Explain how suffering could actually improve an individual's life.

Suffering

The Positives of Suffering

Suffering is any pain, physical or psychological, that is experienced by any man or woman. The causes of suffering vary, some are caused by humans while other types of suffering appear to be due to natural events or may have been caused by God. Some religious believers argue that suffering can be sent by God to either punish or teach humans. Whether this be due to Karma or because of the 'fall of man', many other religious believers would argue that their God does not cause suffering. However, it is also believed that God may allow suffering because humans have brought it upon themselves or can grow in their faith because of their trials.

Types of Suffering

When watching the news, it is easy to spot ways in which people suffer every day. Whether in the UK or outside of it, suffering caused by man or by nature is clear to see. Wars bring great suffering to many innocent people and are always caused by man. They bring obvious pain through death and physical injury but also bring forms of suffering that often last much longer; generations of a family can be killed; homes and buildings are destroyed and take years to be rebuilt. However, the use of chemicals and biological weapons in warfare has a much greater impact. During the Second World War the **atom bomb** was used by the USA in strikes against Japan. The bombs killed thousands on impact but the cancers and illnesses caused by the bomb infected families for years later.

Types of Suffering (cont.)

It is widely understood that 20 per cent of the world's population controls 80 per cent of the world's wealth. This has led to millions of people all over the world living in poverty unable to provide for their basic needs such as food and water. In 2000 the **Jubilee** appeal set to raise awareness of the poverty in the **Third World** and prompt wealthier governments to cancel the debt that they were owed by the poorer countries. This did make some difference but still people all over the world die in their hundreds every day.

Natural disasters such as earthquakes, floods and tsunamis claim thousands of lives all over the world and would seem to occur without any prompting by humans. However, due to poverty, many lives are lost due to poor living conditions and people being forced to live in areas of the world not truly suited to human living. Large areas of Bangladesh are at sea level and are used by many to grow rice to live on. Due to high tides and high rain much of this is flooded regularly with people losing their homes and some their lives. If these people were not poor they would not have to live in these areas, therefore it could be argued that man influences many who die during natural disasters.

In recent times, many of the world's natural disasters have caused the greatest suffering to some of the poorest people. The devastation caused by Hurricane Katrina in New Orleans affects over a million people, many of which were already poor. The damage is still to be fully repaired, meaning that their suffering continues.

✓ Maximise Your Marks

Explaining that suffering is caused by man or by either nature or a god will gain higher marks. To get the highest possible marks, you must demonstrate that man may have more control over suffering than would first appear. Ensure that you can argue that man is capable of both preventing and causing unnecessary suffering.

⚲ Boost Your Memory

In the week before your exam, watch the news carefully and make notes on at least two stories where people are enduring suffering. Note why these are happening, are humans in any way responsible for the suffering and how you can use the information in an exam question.

❓ Test Yourself

1. List types of suffering caused by man.
2. Explain one way in which suffering could be overcome.
3. Do you think there will ever be a time without suffering? Give a reason for your answer.

★ Stretch Yourself

1. 'All suffering is caused by God'. List the arguments in favour and against this statement.
2. Explain how physical suffering can harm an individual's life.

Practice Questions

Complete these exam-style questions to test your understanding. Check your answers on page 92. You may wish to answer these questions on a separate piece of paper.

1 What does one religion teach about caring for others? (4)

2 Describe religious teachings about environmental issues. (5)

3 What arguments might a religious believer use to explain why there is suffering and evil in the world? (3)

4 Explain why a religious believer may support a charity that cares for the poor. (3)

5 Explain why a religious believer might have different views about how to deal with marriage breakdown than a secular person. (4)

6 Explain how a religious believer might work to improve the environment. (5)

....

....

....

....

7 For all of the following questions, explain whether you agree with the statement. You must then give reasons to support your answer and show that you have thought about different points of view. You must refer to the teachings of at least one religion in your answer.

    a) "The death penalty is the only way to deter some people from murder." (4)

....

....

....

....

    b) "I know that there is no god because I see so much suffering." (4)

....

....

....

....

    c) "Marriage is the only place where sex should take place." (4)

....

....

....

....

How well did you do?

| 0–20 | Try again | 21–25 | Getting there | 26–30 | Good work | 31–36 | Excellent! |

Sanctity of Life

What Makes Life Sacred?

Religious believers see that life is given by God and is always special and has its own value. As God has created life, only He has the right to end it, making it sacred. Although this does not apply for a secular person, it does not mean that life is without value but that they have to look elsewhere for values in life.

In Genesis 1, verses 26–27 Christians read:

"So God created man in His own image, in the image of God He created Him; male and female He created them."

Christians use this passage to show that they are separated from the rest of Creation and have been made special and therefore sacred, in God's image. The passage also states that male and females are equal as they were both created in His image. Genesis 2, verse 7 says that God **"breathed into his nostrils the breath of life"**. This verse points to the belief that God creates life and that He began humanity.

✓ Maximise Your Marks

Knowing more than one passage of scripture for religions which teach that life comes from God will gain higher marks.

Practical Terms

Each religion believes that we should all work to protect the lives of those around us, regardless of any discriminating factors. This may lead a religious believer to take up an occupation that does this, such as a doctor or a nurse. As a result of this, the belief may prevent them from fighting in war. In 1 Corinthians 3, verse 16 Paul writes:

"Don't you know that your body is the temple of the Holy Spirit and that God lives in you?"

Although this is obviously a Christian scripture, the essence of it applies to all religions. This is that each life has been created sacred and it is the responsibility of each person to look after what they have been given.

For Muslims, the sanctity of life is a key part of their faith.

"Whosoever has spared the life of a soul, it is as though he has spared the life of all people. Whosoever has killed a soul, it is as though he has murdered all of mankind."
(Qur'an 5, verse 32)

They believe that life is given by Allah and should be both respected and protected because of this.

Sikhs have great respect for life, which is regarded as a gift from **Waheguru**. They too believe, like Christians and Muslims, that life should be protected wherever possible and that it is the greatest gift given to them.

When Might it be Applied?

If each life is sacred, then anything that ends life early or alters life in some way is likely to cause concern. An abortion is when a pregnancy is intentionally terminated before term. Regardless of the reason for an abortion, religious believers would have a difficult decision to make as to whether abortion would be the right course of action to take. Christians also believe that life begins at conception:

"You created every part of me, you put me together in my Mother's womb." (Psalm 139:13)

Muslim views depend upon at what stage of the pregnancy the abortion is planned for, but the decision is still not taken lightly. Jews have very strict views on abortion. Rabbis teach that abortion is equal to murder, stating that life in the womb is the same as life outside of it. They do however argue that life is fully granted after

40 days of the pregnancy. Therefore, some Jewish people believe that abortion during the first 40 days after conception is acceptable.

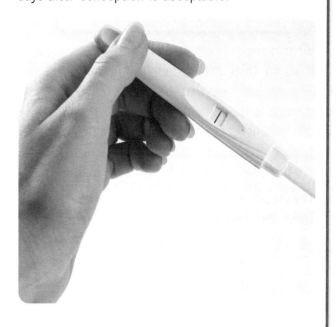

Embryology and Euthanasia

Embryology is the use of embryos in scientific research to try and find cures for diseases and illnesses. It could be argued that potential life has been ended for these tests to take place. In addition, even if an embryo is seen as the potential for life, many religious believers could argue that life is not being protected and not valued in the way that a gift from God should be.

In most cases, euthanasia allows an individual the chance to end their life, usually if they are unable to commit suicide. This clearly sees a life being ended prematurely, going against the

sanctity of life principle. The four major world religions object to **active euthanasia**, with Sikhs following the teaching about Sewa and caring for others suggests that they should care for somebody in need rather than condoning the ending of their life.

✓ Maximise Your Marks

You need to be able to demonstrate the positive and negative impact that the sanctity of life principle could have if applied universally.

❓ Test Yourself

1. State one reason why life might be sacred.

2. Name any situations where life could be seen as not being sacred.

3. What situations could the sanctity of life be applied to?

4. How does the UK show value for life?

⭐ Stretch Yourself

1. Describe one way in which UK laws could be changed to promote the sanctity of life.

2. Why could it be impossible to apply the sanctity of life principle in law?

When Does Life Begin?

Is Birth the Start of Life?

What is life? In both religious and secular views there are three main beliefs as to when life starts. From the moment that the egg is fertilised through to the birth of a child there are great discussions as to when that life becomes human. Is pregnancy simply the 'potential' for life? There are three key beliefs as to when life does start.

At conception

Most **Christians** believe that God is a significant part of the process and that He gives life at the start of the pregnancy.

The moment that the sperm cell fertilises the egg, is called conception. Most Christians and **Jews** believe that at this moment God is present and involved in the creation of life.

"For you created my inmost being; you knit me together in my mother's womb."
(Psalm 139, verse 13)

Sikhs also believe that life begins at conception and that the soul is given to the body.

"In the mother's womb, life was enshrined and cherished. You were blessed with body and soul."
(Guru Arjan, page 1004, Line 13)

After 24 hours, the egg begins to divide and form more and more cells. This happens extremely quickly. The egg is known as a **zygote** (the specific name given to the 'baby' between conception and 12 days), with the cell dividing and growing to become a **blastocyst**.

After 120 days

This time of pregnancy is sometimes known as the '**quickening**' and is of particular significance to **Muslims** and some Christians. At this stage, the mother can start to feel the embryo move in the womb and the embryo is almost fully formed with the heart beating strongly. As the baby is now showing clear signs of active life, the belief is that God has now given it its soul and life has begun.

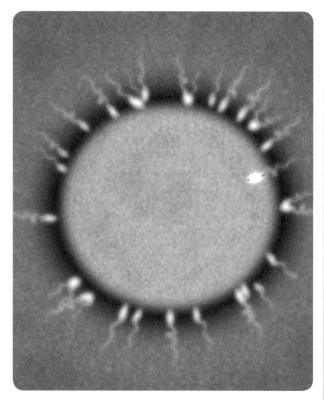

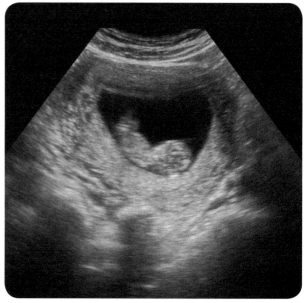

Is Birth the Start of Life? (cont.)

At birth

A commonly held belief is that life begins when a baby is born. This is primarily a **secular** view although some religious believers will accept it too. The belief is based around the fact that after birth the baby becomes independent of its mother and, therefore, has full life. UK law recognises that life begins at birth and that the baby does not have equal human rights until it has been born. For example, the laws on abortion allow a pregnancy to be terminated in the interests of the woman as they are viewed to be more important than that of the foetus.

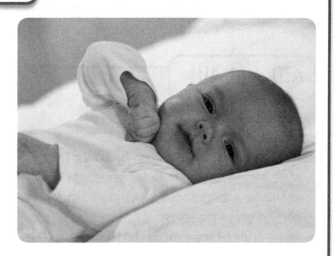

It is clear that during pregnancy a foetus needs the mother to survive, but advances in medical techniques and knowledge have clouded the issue as to when life begins. Premature babies now have a much higher chance of survival than they have ever done in the past. However, they cannot survive without medical intervention, yet UK law recognises that they have full human rights equivalent to a baby born at full term.

🔘 Boost Your Memory

Practice how to explain your view as to when life starts. Make sure you refer to the teaching of a least one religion and how your view compares to it.

Ethics

Legal Implications

The question of the start of life has many implications. In a court of law, the UK recognises that life starts at birth. This means that if a pregnant woman is assaulted and the baby dies, then the crime committed is assault. However, if the UK adopted the Christian belief as to the start of life then the crime could well be considered to be **murder** or **manslaughter**.

✓ Maximise Your Marks

An easy way to gain higher marks is to make sure you know when each stage of life happens. Use the correct terms and describe how they relate to UK law. You also need to evaluate all three beliefs relating to abortion carefully, work out which one your view is closest to and explain what has brought you to this opinion.

❓ Test Yourself

1. Why do most Christians believe that life starts at conception?

2. What is the name given to the stage of pregnancy at 120 days?

3. When does UK law seem to recognise that 'life' begins?

4. What are the different names given to a baby throughout pregnancy?

⭐ Stretch Yourself

1. Draw a small table to show the different religious views on the start of life and explain the similarities and differences.

2. Describe the different views that the quote 'an embryo is only the potential for life' would prompt.

In Vitro Fertilisation

AID and AIH

In Vitro Fertilisation (IVF) falls into two categories; either **AID** or **AIH**.

- **AID – Artificial Insemination by Donor** The male partner is unable to provide suitable sperm for a pregnancy to take place, so a third party donates the sperm.
- **AIH – Artificial Insemination by Husband** The man may have a low sperm count or other complications exist but his sperm are still healthy.

In vitro comes from the Greek meaning 'in glass'. The egg is fertilised with either the partner's sperm or that of a donor and then inserted into an egg from the female in a laboratory, the egg is then planted inside the womb. More than one egg is often fertilised to increase the chances of a pregnancy being successful.

Playing God

If a couple cannot have children naturally should they have them at all? Did God intend for them not to have children? If someone does not believe in God, then they will probably not consider these viewpoints and would most likely see it as their right to receive IVF. In the UK, most couples are able to have their first treatment at the expense of the NHS but then have to pay for further treatments if this is unsuccessful.

Religious Teaching

The Christian Church has responded clearly to the ethical discussion on IVF. All have explained that IVF is suitable in some circumstances but not in all. **The Roman Catholic Church** believes that IVF is only acceptable in the following circumstances:

- No 'spare embryos' are created.
- No third parties are used.
- They do not replace sex within a marriage.
- **AI** is acceptable, only if the husband's sperm is used.
- **AID** is not acceptable as it requires the sperm of another man, who is not the husband. For the Catholic Church, this is seen as the same as adultery.

Pope Pius XII went as far as to say that AID is **'mechanical adultery'**, due to the fact that the sperm of a man outside of the marriage was being used to conceive.

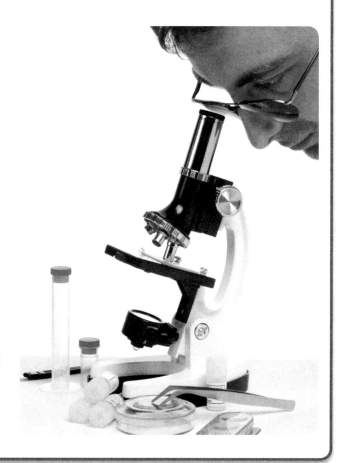

Religious Teaching (cont.)

The **Church of England** has taken a far more relaxed stance on the issue as they argue that IVF is acceptable in all its forms, including the donation of eggs and sperm by third parties. Experimenting on 'spare' human embryos is acceptable up to 14 days after fertilisation, because up to 14 days a foetus can split into two and form twins.

The **Methodist Church** is largely in agreement with the Church of England, stating that it is right for scientists to try to learn more about causes and cures of infertility, but only up to 14 days after fertilisation.

Muslims only support AIH, as they feel that the involvement of a third party undermines the marriage. Like the Catholic Church, they also view it as adultery. **Sikhs** are happy for IVF to take place but are wary of the impact that it can have on the family, especially in the case of AID.

For **Jews**, IVF offers couples a chance to be blessed by God. Therefore, IVF is absolutely necessary for a couple if it is available and should not be turned down. Jews also believe that the selective reduction of a multiple pregnancy is acceptable if it increases the chance of life continuing.

Surrogacy and Adoption

When IVF does not work, **surrogacy** can be considered. Here, another woman carries the pregnancy, which may have been fertilised by either the partner or donor sperm. In many countries, like the USA, a woman may be paid to be a surrogate mother. This is against the law in the UK, where only a gift can be given not a payment. All Churches agree that surrogacy is wrong because:
* It involves a third party in a much bigger way than sperm.
* It can create massive problems for everyone concerned, including the child.

All religions agree that a suitable alternative to IVF is **adoption**, even though there are obvious issues associated with it.

Concerns always exist as to whether the couple can fully accept the child as their own and as to how the child will react when they learn that their parents are not their biological parents. However, all religions argue that they can support people in this situation to strengthen the family.

✓ Maximise Your Marks

To gain higher marks, you need to show that you can demonstrate the harm that using IVF can cause in all circumstances and whether these outweigh the possible benefits.

Ethics

? Test Yourself

1. What is the difference between AID and AIH?
2. Why may IVF harm a family?
3. Why are multiple eggs used in the treatment?
4. Explain why surrogacy may be a bad idea.

★ Stretch Yourself

1. Compare the strengths and weaknesses of adoption with IVF.
2. Why might a religious believer be against the use of embryos in scientific testing?

Abortion

UK Laws on Abortion

The laws on abortion in the UK have remained relatively the same since the **Abortion Act of 1967** was passed through Parliament.

The bill set out guidelines as to when an abortion can be allowed and on what grounds. An abortion is defined as the intentional termination of a pregnancy with medical assistance.

For a woman to be granted an abortion, **two doctors** have to agree that she has just cause to undergo the operation. Reasons for being allowed to have an abortion include showing that the pregnancy may cause the mother serious physical or psychological harm; proving that the woman's other children would be negatively affected by the birth of another baby; or tests showing that the foetus may suffer from a disability from birth.

These rules apply up to the first 24 weeks of a pregnancy. From this point on abortions are usually only allowed in extreme cases where the possible harm to the mother can be proven to be significant. A woman may be denied an abortion if she has had numerous previous abortions. However, these are often not referred to as abortions but a 'still birth' as the baby is induced.

UK Laws on Embryos

Over the last 20 years there have been many changes in UK law and practice with regards to abortion and embryos.

Embryology Act 1990
Scientists were allowed to create embryos outside of the womb and store them legally for the first time. The pregnancy stage limit for abortions in normal circumstances was reduced from 28 weeks to 24 weeks.

Human Fertilisation and Embryology Act (Ongoing)
- 2006 – screenings of embryos were introduced to show abnormalities in pregnancy, raising the likelihood of more abortions.
- 2007 – women were given the right to donate their eggs to scientific research, raising questions about the 'potential' of life.

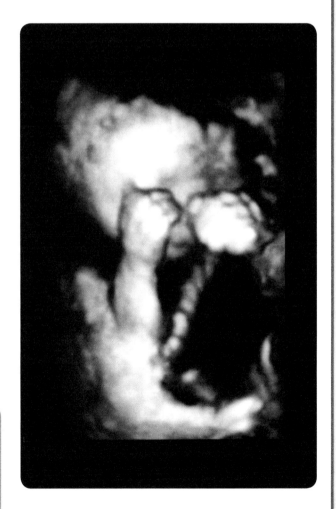

💡 Boost Your Memory

Create a flowchart to show how laws on abortion have changed. Highlight the three changes that you think have been the most significant. You may want to include how changes in medical science have helped to prolong the life of prematurely born babies.

Abortions Compared to Foetus Development

The medical procedures used to terminate a pregnancy vary greatly dependent upon the stage that the pregnancy has reached. At conception, there is the chance that twins can form. This happens when either two eggs are fertilised or one egg splits, forming non-identical and identical twins respectively. At this point the DNA is formed and this acts as the design for the life of the embryo.

Although not all agree, some religious believers argue that the **Morning After Pill** is the first type of abortion. The pill is taken up to three days after a woman thinks she may have become pregnant and stops a fertilised egg from attaching itself to the womb and induces a period.

Up to the eighth week of pregnancy the woman can be given **Suction Aspiration** which requires the use of a powerful vacuum, used under anaesthetic, to remove the foetus through the vagina. At this stage, the foetus is about the size of a kidney bean and some features such as fingers are starting to form.

After the 12th week until the 16th week **Dilation and Curettage** has be to used and is a more invasive procedure where the pregnancy is terminated using a surgical knife before being removed.

Between the 16th and the 20th week a saline injection is given to the foetus, killing it inside the womb, before the womb goes through the process of child birth to remove the foetus from the mother's body. After this stage surgical tools may be required to help the mother deliver the foetus. Sometimes the foetus may still be alive when it is born.

Ethics

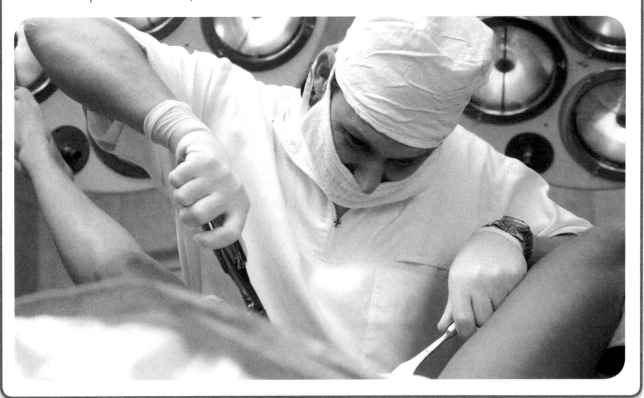

❓ Test Yourself

1 What is an abortion?

2 Why do many Christians think that abortions should be avoided?

3 When might a religious believer allow an abortion?

⭐ Stretch Yourself

1 UK laws on abortion clearly favour the wishes of the pregnant woman. Explain the advantages and disadvantages of this position.

Views on Abortion

Pro-Life

People who argue in favour of pro-life state that the foetus has a right to life and should be protected from harm wherever possible. They argue that the foetus is not simply the potential for life but already has life and can be viewed as human.

"Before I formed you in the womb I knew you, before you were born I set you apart." (Jeremiah 1, verse 5)

They put forward the argument that if the pregnancy is unwanted, then it should not be terminated but when born, the baby should be given up for adoption. Some pro-life supporters may allow abortions in some limited cases, such as if the woman has been raped or if the pregnancy was not planned and could seriously physically harm the mother. However, they may still state that adoption is a better option in the case of a rape victim. Many pro-life supporters are religious believers, most notably Christians who argue that life begins at conception not birth.

"For you created my inmost being; you knit me together in my mother's womb." (Psalm 139, verse 13)

Pro-Choice

Pro-choice supporters focus their beliefs and arguments on the rights of the mother and not of the foetus. They state that the woman should be able to make the decision as to what to do with the pregnancy as it is her body and the pregnancy is simply part of her. They often argue that life begins at birth and before then the foetus simply has the potential for human life and is not fully human until it is born.

There are only a small number of religious believers who support the pro-choice movement, these include the Church of England who are likely to see the act as the 'lesser of two evils'. Also, Muslims argue that life begins at 120 days of the pregnancy so will consider abortions before this point, as long as it can be proven that it is the best possible solution for the mother, the pregnancy and the mother's family.

✔ Maximise Your Marks

Ensure that for whichever religion you have studied you can quote at least two verses relate closely to views on abortion. Where possible, try to also remember exactly where the quotes come from. List what you think are the three strongest reasons in support of abortion and the three strongest reasons against abortion. Now try and argue those points against each other to create a strong argument either in favour or against abortion.

The Right of the Father

The Embryology Act of 1990 stated that only the pregnant woman should be able to request an abortion. Because of this, the act also stated that the father had no right to either propose an abortion or prevent it from happening. Religious believers would generally state that any decision should be made by the couple.

This clearly shows that UK law views the mother's rights and views as being higher than of the father. This can cause serious issues in a relationship and the decision to have an abortion could lead to the breakdown of the relationship.

Is Adoption a Good Alternative?

Many pro-life supporters see adoption as a sensible alternative to abortion. They argue that not only does it prevent a life from being ended but it also allows a couple to have a child where they might not have otherwise been able to.

However, it could be argued that this does not really offer much help to the pregnant woman. She will still have to continue the pregnancy for its natural duration and may then struggle to 'give up' the baby at birth. It would also only be helpful for pregnancies where the woman would not suffer any physical or psychological trauma.

Effects of Abortion

Besides the obvious affect of the pregnancy coming to an end, there are further issues that may occur because of an abortion. In some rare cases the woman can be physically harmed by the abortion procedure. This may cause complications in any further pregnancies. Much more common than this though, is the chance that the woman may suffer emotional difficulties after she has undergone the abortion.

In these cases, women have recounted experiences of grief, where they feel that they have lost something. This is largely due to the fact that their body knows that it was pregnant and no longer is.

In extension to this, the existing family may also be affected. They could be suffering from the potential addition of another member to the family, but younger members of the family may struggle to understand why an abortion has to take place.

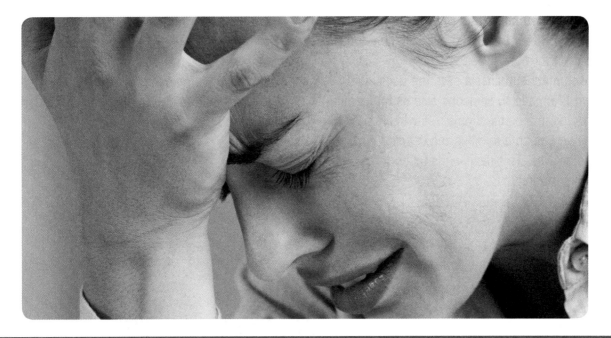

Ethics

❓ Test Yourself

1. Would a pro-choice believer be for or against abortion?
2. Is a religious believer likely to be a pro-choice or pro-life believer?

⭐ Stretch Yourself

1. Explain what you think are the two strongest arguments to support abortions and the two strongest arguments against the use of abortions.

Euthanasia

Who Decides When we Should Die?

Do we as humans have the right to decide when our lives should end? If we are physically able we could end our own lives but if not, should euthanasia be available to us?

Types of Euthanasia

Although all forms of euthanasia see a human life being brought to an end, the UK law states that the circumstances and actions are of high importance. There are two main groups that euthanasia fall into.

Active euthanasia includes all cases where a medical professional provides the patient with a chemical substance to end their life early. For example, a person who is terminally ill and in a lot of pain is given a lethal injection. Active euthanasia is split into two categories:

- **Voluntary euthanasia** is when a person asks for their life to be ended but may be unable to do it for themselves.
- **Involuntary euthanasia** sees the decision to end life made by someone else as the person may be in a coma or only a few hours old so they are unable to make the decision for themselves. This decision is taken to end suffering.

Passive euthanasia only happens when treatment that is keeping a patient alive is removed. For example, a patient in a paralysed state has their life support machine turned off. This can only be done with either their consent or the consent of the family and the agreement of a doctor.

Euthanasia should not be confused with '**assisted suicide**'. Assisted suicide takes place without the guidance of a medical professional and often involves a family member or close friend helping someone to die, for example suffocating someone with a pillow.

UK Laws on Euthanasia

The law in the United Kingdom is very clear in terms of euthanasia; the removal of treatment that is prolonging life, passive euthanasia, is legal.

However, any form of active euthanasia is illegal. It is also illegal for any UK citizen to help someone else leave the country so that they can end their life early in somewhere like Switzerland. Even though someone may write a **living will** that states their desire to end their life and gives permission for this to happen, if they are assisted in their desire to die, it is often still seen that murder has been committed. If active euthanasia was legalised it could start a **slippery slope** that would make life disposable and lead to more able people losing their lives.

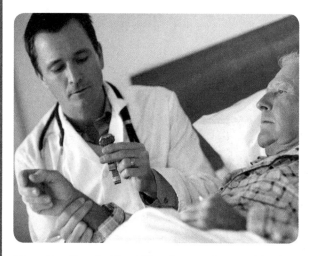

The situation in the UK raises serious ethical dilemmas for families with elderly or critically ill relatives. They would probably not want to break the law but would want to do all that they can to ease the suffering of their loved ones.

Alternatives to Euthanasia

The hospice movement has provided those nearing the end of their lives with the opportunity to make the most of their final days. Many hospices are run by **Christians** as they believe that it offers a viable alternative to euthanasia and shows care in someone's time of need.

"The LORD gave and the Lord has taken away." (Job 1, verse 21)

Hospices care for people of any age not just the elderly and are not to be confused with residential homes. Organisations like **Make a Wish** also give individuals the opportunity for children between the ages of four and 17 to do something special as they deal with a terminal illness. As medical advances continue, patients may be given the option of euthanasia but may recover or a new treatment found. Religious believers would also argue that miracles happen and these could take place in a hospice, with someone being restored to full health.

💡 Boost Your Memory

Research a local hospice near to where you live. Note down their mission statement; who funds them and who the hospice helps.

✓ Maximise Your Marks

Ensure that you can show how the legalisation of euthanasia could have a greater impact on the value of life.

Other Options

Not everyone agrees with the hospice movement. Although a hospice may make someone's life more comfortable, should they be kept alive? People who run hospices may be seen as trying to '**play God**', as the person in the hospice is perhaps ready to die. The care given by the hospice may extend the life of an individual who would otherwise have died earlier. This argument can also be used for keeping someone alive using life support machines, when without them they would die naturally. However, under the **Hippocratic Oath**, doctors promise to preserve life and care for their patients. Would euthanasia go against this?

Although euthanasia clearly relieves the pain that the patient is suffering, their life has to end for this to happen.

❓ Test Yourself

1 Under what conditions is euthanasia legal in the UK?

2 Who must be involved in the action of ending someone's life for it to be classed as legal?

3 Why would a religious believer support the work of a hospice?

4 What does the term 'playing God' mean?

⭐ Stretch Yourself

1 See how many arguments in favour and against euthanasia you can think of. Does this have any influence on your opinion? Why?

2 'The hospice movement does not provide much hope for a dying child.' Explain the different views that the quote might raise.

Animal Rights

Animals as Food

For many, eating meat is completely normal, whether they be religious believers or not. However, for others some animals or all animals should not be consumed, as commanded in scripture. Many Christians believe that they are instructed by God to eat meat in **Genesis 1, verse 28** when they are instructed to subdue the Earth. However, other Christians feel that this passage simply tells them that they should look after the Earth and not necessarily eat meat. Views in other religions vary greatly. Jews are allowed to eat meat as long as they have been killed according to **Kosher** or **Shechita** law. This prevents the meat from being classed as being unclean.

Both Muslims and Sikhs believe that eating animals for food is permissible. However, they disagree greatly in the consumption of **Halal** meat. Muslims use the process of draining the blood from the animal as this makes it clean to eat. For Sikhs, this causes the animal far too much pain and distress so is not allowed. Some Sikhs also choose to be vegetarian due to their Hindu heritage and belief about the close links between animals and gods, especially the cow.

> ### Boost Your Memory
>
> Use the word animals to create yourself a memorable acrostic to cover the key points listed above. For example, Allah Never Intended Man to Allow Lots of Suffering.

Animal Testing

Medical Testing

Vivisection sees animals tested upon to try and find cures for a range of illnesses and diseases. A wide range of animals are used to both test new drugs on and also to be exposed to different illnesses. The reaction that the animals have is used to help extend understanding and develop cures for humans. **Isaiah 11, verse 6–8** teaches Christians that they should co-exist with animals and that animals and the Earth should not be exploited. **Roman Catholics** are taught that animals are below humans and that they should not place too much importance on them, therefore allowing them to be used in experiments. Other denominations teach that animals should not be abused and some Christians interpret this as making vivisection unethical.

Muslims are taught that experimentation to help cure diseases is permissible as long as the animal does not experience any undue suffering. Jews are taught through the **Talmud** that animals should be treated well, although they can be used to ease the suffering of humans. As Sikhs believe in **reincarnation**, they believe that they or their loved ones may return in another life as an animal. Because of this they want to avoid all unnecessary harm to animals but do allow experimentation where it may benefit humans.

Cosmetic Testing

Views on cosmetic testing being carried out on animals usually provokes more objections than when testing is carried out for medical reasons. All religious believers are likely to have more objections to animal testing for cosmetic reasons than they do for medical reasons. This is due to all religions teaching their followers that animals should not be made to endure any undue suffering. Many **multi-national companies** also object to cosmetic testing on animals. Shops like the Body Shop and Boots, ensure that their products are tested on humans and not on animals.

Implications of Animal Testing

Many chemicals and drugs that have been tested on animals have later been shown to cause different reactions when used by humans. Here are a few examples:

- The **contraceptive pill** can cause blood clots in humans yet has the opposite effect on dogs.
- **Morphine** helps humans to sleep yet excites cats.
- **Asprin** is a human painkiller yet causes birth defects in mice.

Many other cases show that humans and animals can be too dissimilar. The charity Animal Aid, has produced much literature showing these issues. These include the testing of rats informed scientists that humans did not need Vitamin C. Testing on animals produced results that suggested alcohol did not cause liver damage and that smoking did not cause cancer. Testing on humans has shown these not to be the case.

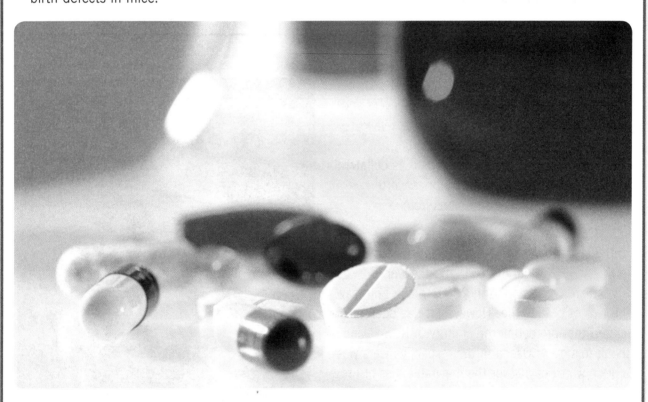

✓ Maximise Your Marks

To gain higher marks, you must be able to show the value of testing on animals whilst also being able to clearly show why many disagree with testing on animals for any reason.

❓ Test Yourself

1. What is vivisection?
2. What type of animal testing are religions more likely to support?
3. Why might animal testing not be helpful?
4. Give two reasons why a religious believer may disagree with animal testing.

⭐ Stretch Yourself

1. Explain why some Sikhs might choose to become vegetarian.
2. List the reasons why anyone might object to eating meat.

War and Peace

War

War is violence between two or more armies. These armies may be from different countries or from the same one. If they are from the same country then this is called a **civil war**.

Death always takes place in war and the causalities almost always include **civilians** who have not chosen to fight.

Is Killing Always Wrong?

In every war throughout history, innocent people have lost their lives. Many religious believers and secular people have argued that this is a valid reason to suggest that all wars are wrong. However, what is sometimes regarded as **collateral damage** is sometimes seen as a price worth paying to prevent other situations from developing.

In the last two decades, the UK has been involved in the first Gulf War in 1990 and the war in Afghanistan that started in 2001, which both saw the loss of civilian life. However, it has been argued that protecting the country of Kuwait and trying to stop Al Qaeda in the respective wars was a price worth paying for the inevitable loss of life.

Religious War

Although many religious believers argue that violence is wrong, there are occasions where some feel that fighting is necessary. These times are known as **Holy Wars**, or **Jihads**.

Christians base much of their teaching and thinking on the work of St Thomas Aquinas in the 13th Century. He theorised about various conditions that a just war must meet and he eventually settled on a list of seven criteria that he believed must be met for it to be fair and therefore classed as a **Just War**:

- The war must be for a just cause.
- The war must be lawfully declared by a lawful authority.
- The intention behind the war must be good.
- All other ways of resolving the problem should have been tried first.
- There must be a reasonable chance of success.
- The means used to fight the war must be proportionate with the aims that are trying to be achieved.
- The war must bring about more good than the harm that it causes.

Jihad

Jihad means 'struggle' and falls into two categories: **Greater Jihad** and **Lesser Jihad**. A greater Jihad is fought on a daily basis by the whole of the Muslim community. They believe that they must stand against the evil influences that exist in the world and hold strong together in their faith. It is the internal battle that every Muslim struggles with every day to live a good life. The lesser Jihad has to be declared by a spiritual authority within Islam, and is often against an individual. These are brought about to protect the religion. An example of this was when a Jihad was declared against a Danish newspaper and its cartoonists, after a cartoon was printed suggesting a link with Muhammad and terrorists in 2005.

There are two reasons where a lesser Jihad can be declared. Any Muslim must be willing to defend their faith from an outside force and are called a '**Mujahid**' when they take up arms. They must also be willing to take up arms when they witness any social injustice against Muslims and non-Muslims alike. However, like with Just War, other criteria must also apply. A Jihad has to come as a last resort as suffering should be avoided where possible. Unlike the teachings of Jesus, Muslims are not taught to turn the other cheek and must stand up to defend weaker members of their community.

Milchemet Mitzvah

In Jewish teaching some wars are seen as being obligatory, meaning that Jews must be willing to fight in them. In Joshua 1, verses 2–6 Jews are instructed by God to stand and fight for the Promised Land. This principle has then been applied to other situations in which Jews have found themselves. They can fight when:

- The enemy has struck first.
- A pre-emptive strike is necessary to prevent the loss of Jewish lives (this has added to the conflict in Palestine between Israelis and Palestinians).
- Jews feel that they are being called by God to fight.

Any wars outside of the above criteria are known as **Milchemet Reshut**, or 'optional war'.

For this to happen there must also be good cause. The war must meet the following conditions:
- All other alternatives have been tried but have failed.
- The war is fought between armies to keep civilian causalities to a minimum.
- Any damage to land or property during the war is kept to a minimum.

This shows that there are many similarities between the beliefs of Christians, Muslims and Jews when it comes to war and when fighting should be permitted.

> ### ✓ Maximise Your Marks
>
> To gain higher marks, ensure that you can explain the similarities and differences between a Just War and a Lesser Jihad.

❓ Test Yourself

1. Explain the difference between a Jihad and a Just War.
2. List which you think are the three strongest reasons for war.
3. List three reasons why war may not be a bad thing.

⭐ Stretch Yourself

1. Show how war can bring about good as well as bad.
2. Describe how a recent war relates to a religion that you have studied and their theory as to whether it should have been fought or not.

Views on War and Peace

Should Everyone Fight?

Many people choose not to fight at times of war. They either choose to be **pacifists** or **conscientious objectors**. Although neither group fight they have different attitudes as to what part they will take. A pacifist takes the view that all involvement in war is wrong, regardless of whether any harm could come from their participation. During the Second World War, thousands of men and women lost their lives by supporting soldiers as first aid officers, with one of their responsibilities being to try and rescue injured soldiers on the front line.

A conscientious objector will refuse to act violently but is willing to support a war effort in peaceful ways. Again during the first and second world wars conscientious objectors volunteered as members of the medical staff and many lost their lives trying to rescue injured soldiers from the battlefield.

Human Rights and Amnesty International

During times of war it is often difficult to protect the rights of individuals, whether they be soldiers or civilians. In 1948 the **United Nations** published the **Universal Declaration of Human Rights**, which was designed to protect people at times of war and outside of war. The declaration set out 30 'articles' to ensure that individuals were protected from harm under law. All UN nations agreed to these articles and agreed to support their implementation. The articles protect basic human rights and aim to stop persecution, whilst allowing freedom of movement and freedom of speech.

Amnesty International was founded in 1961 by a British lawyer called Peter Benenson after he read about social injustice in Portugal. Since then the organisation has sought to add to the work of the UN declaration and actively protect individuals and groups who have been wrongly treated by a government or regime. Its main aims are closely related to war, although they may sometimes be acted on outside of war. The organisation is committed to:
- freeing prisoners of conscience
- gaining fair trial for political prisoners
- ending torture, political killings and 'disappearances'
- abolishing the death penalty throughout the world

The work of Amnesty International has been recognised all over the world, with it being awarded the **Nobel Peace Prize** in 1977 and the **United Nations Human Rights Prize** in 1978.

Religious Teaching

In the Old Testament, people are sometimes commanded by God to go to war. In Deuteronomy, Joshua and Judges, God often tells His people to fight and destroy foreign tribes to gain the Promised Land (Israel).

"The lord your God will drive out those nations before you, little by little … the Lord your God will deliver them over to you, throwing them into great confusion until they are destroyed … no one will be able to stand up against you; you will destroy them." (Deuteronomy 7, verses 22–24)

The Old Testament prophet, Joel, tells the people that God wants them to go and fight.

"Prepare for war! Rouse the warriors! Let all the fighting men draw near and attack."
(Joel 3, verses 9–10)

Christians use these quotes in a discussion about war and the use of violence to show that there are times when war is justified. God cannot be totally opposed to war in all circumstances.

To some Christians this means that it can sometimes be right to be violent when people are being cheated or treated unfairly. During His teaching, Jesus made references to violence and to tools of war. In Matthew 10, verses 34–36, Jesus talks about families being separated and His word being a sword not peace.

Some Christians interpret this as Jesus showing that division is permissible and that if violence is required then it can be used. However, when the passage is read in context (the verses before and after are read too) then many other Christians argue that the message that Jesus is bringing is what will divide families. This is because His teachings are different from the Jewish faith and will make members of the same family choose which religion they believe in.

Ethics

✓ Maximise Your Marks

To gain the highest marks in this section you must show the value and damage that war brings. With this you must be able to show that you understand how religion has been involved in war throughout history, explaining when it may have been right and wrong for it to do so.

❓ Test Yourself

1. Why might someone choose to be a conscientious objector?
2. When was Amnesty International founded?

⭐ Stretch Yourself

1. Explain the reasons why a religious believer should not go to war.

Prejudice and Discrimination

Are Prejudice and Discrimination the Same?

Prejudices are the ideas that we may have about other people that are based on a stereotype and make us think differently about some without good reason. If we then choose to act on these thoughts in some way then we are discriminating. So prejudice is in our mind and discrimination is when we act on these thoughts.

The Main Types of Prejudice and Discrimination

Racism has seen millions of people treated differently because of the colour of their skin or because of their country of origin, with one notable case being **Apartheid** in South Africa. **Sexism** has seen men and women divided throughout history, with women often being seen as lesser than men. **Poverty** is a big cause of discrimination, with people treated poorly because they have less money or come from a poorer background. Another notable prejudice exists towards people who have either **physical disabilities** or **learning difficulties**. **Homophobia** has become a big issue in recent decades, with gay men or lesbians victimised because of their sexuality.

Good Samaritan

The parable of the Good Samaritan appears in Luke (10, verses 25–37). Jesus teaches about a Jewish traveller who is beaten, robbed, and left to die. First a priest and then a Levite come by, but both avoid the man. After these a Samaritan walks by and helps the traveller. At the time, Jews despised Samaritans as they saw them as being unclean. Jesus used this example to show that all people should treat each other equally, regardless of where they come from. This teaching can be applied to all differences not just race.

Influential People

Martin Luther King Jr was instrumental in the ending of separation between whites and blacks in the USA. The movement of blacks was restricted while that of whites was not. The bus system made blacks give up their seats for a white person.

This was important for the movement because in 1962 **Rosa Parks**, a 42 year old black lady, refused to give up her seat on a bus, leading to a boycotting of the bus system by the black community. King strived for non-violent protest and in 1963 delivered his '**I have a dream**' speech in Washington. A year later, he was awarded the Nobel Peace Prize for his work, before being assassinated in 1968.

Mother Teresa fought to overcome the issue of poverty. Born in 1910, she spent over 45 years working with the poor and sick in Calcutta, India. She showed the world that all people should be treated equally regardless of their background and that those with more should help those with less. In 1979 she was awarded the Nobel Peace Prize and then in 1980 the Bharat Ratna, India's highest civilian honour.

Religion Discrimination

The world's major religions teach the principle of the 'Golden Rule'. It teaches that each person should behave in a way that they would expect to be treated. For Christians, Luke 10, verse 27 reads: 'Love your neighbour as you love yourself'. The Prophet Muhammad taught Muslims:

"None of you truly believes, until he wishes for his brothers what he wishes for himself."

If religions believe the same thing, why do they have different ways of saying it? Each religion believes that its teaching and wording is correct, even though this would seem to separate them.

Religious Teaching

The Roman Catholic Church and the Church of England have both stated that only men can hold positions of authority in the Church. However, in some Church of England churches, this view has been relaxed and there is a strong movement in favour of allowing women to become Bishops. However, it is still often the case that men hold the vast majority of positions of authority.

Sikhs believe that all men are equal and should be treated that way, even if they are not Sikhs. After every service at the gurdwara, the congregation share a meal in the langar, taking it in turns to prepare and serve the food. This means that richer people are often serving people with less than they have.

Muslims base their belief about the treatment of others on two key quotes from Allah:

"Allah does not look upon your outward appearance; He looks upon your hearts and your deeds."

(This shows it is wrong to judge on appearances.)

"All of you descend from Adam ... there is no superiority for an Arab over a non-Arab."

(This shows that all people are equal in value.)

✓ Maximise Your Marks

Ensure that you know as many types of discrimination as possible and have a case study in mind for each of them.

Ethics

? Test Yourself

1. Name five types of discrimination.
2. Explain how discrimination might be shown.
3. Describe the problems discrimination might cause.
4. Suggest how discrimination could be dealt with.

★ Stretch Yourself

1. Show how just one individual can make a huge difference.
2. Explain how religions may be viewed as being discriminatory.

Drugs

Prescribed Drugs

Most religions believe that the use of prescription drugs is in the best interests of its members. It can be argued that we have been given the ability by God to develop our scientific and medical knowledge to ease suffering through the use of complex drugs and treatments. One of the main exceptions to this are Jehovah's Witnesses who believe that some prescription drugs are not natural and therefore could alter the body that God has given to them.

Reasons for Drug Taking

In many cases people who decide to use drugs do not intend to become addicted but this is an obvious consequence of use. Many people **experiment** with drugs when they are teenagers. They may not fully understand the dangers of the drugs they are trying but more often it is because they have been offered them by a friend; this is known as **peer pressure**. It is common for a smoker to try **cannabis** in one of their cigarettes, because of the 'high' that it gives and its ease of availability. The problem is that this can start a **slippery slope**. They find the high given by the use of cannabis is no longer strong enough so they use other **harder** drugs, maybe tablets like ecstasy or alternatively something like **amphetamines**.

Older people may start using drugs because of circumstances. If someone is suffering from a painful condition, such as arthritis, they may use cannabis to ease this pain. If they are **depressed**, which may have a number of causes, drugs are sometimes used to help the user to **escape** the feelings that they have.

Illegal Drugs

The **Drugs Act of 2005** in the UK sought to clarify punishments for drug use and possession and to reinforce the classifications of the **1971 Misuse of Drugs Act**. Illegal drugs are split into three categories with A being the worst.

- **Class A:** cocaine and crack (a form of cocaine), ecstasy, heroin, LSD, methadone, methamphetamine (crystal meth), magic mushrooms containing ester of psilocin and any Class B drug which is injected
- **Class B:** amphetamine (not methamphetamine), barbiturates, codeine and cannabis
- **Class C:** anabolic steroids and minor tranquillisers

Punishments for drug use and possession vary greatly, dependent upon the 'class' of drug and also the quantity. If caught in possession, an individual has to prove that the amount that they have is for personal use or they may be charged with '**an intent to supply**' as well as the crime of possession. These punishments range from a **police caution** through to a long prison sentence. In other countries, such as China, anyone found with over 50g of drugs on their person could be sentenced to death.

✔ Maximise Your Marks

Research the five illegal drugs that are used the most in the UK. List the harm that each one can cause to the individual using them and those around them.

The Religious Views

All Christians have generally the same attitudes towards drugs. With Christians viewing the human body as being '**the temple of the Holy Spirit**' (1 Corinthians 6, verse 19), any intentional damage done to it is often seen as being a sin. Simply, the use of any illegal drugs would not be supported by Christians but they would seek to help somebody who was using them.

The Muslim view is very similar to the Christian view. They too believe that the use of drugs is wrong and that it goes against the will of Allah.

"**O You who believe! Intoxicants and gambling, (dedication of) stones and (divination by) arrows are an abomination of Satan's handiwork. Avoid (such abominations) that you may prosper.**" (Surah 5, verse 90)

The term intoxicant relates to alcohol but is also seen by Muslims as including any form of illegal drug. Muslims believe that drugs are a tool of Satan to steer people away from their faith and their belief in the teachings of Allah.

The Sikh Code of Conduct was published in 1950. It provides details of how Sikhs should live. It bans the use of tobacco, cannabis, opium, cocaine and alcohol or any other substance that can affect the mind and so prevent a Sikh from being able to worship properly. However, a Sikh can smoke or drink but must ensure that all traces of either item are removed from their body before entering a gurdwara.

Jews are opposed to the use of drugs not prescribed by a doctor. However, alcohol is present in wine, which plays an important part in many Jewish services. Therefore, it can be drunk but not to excess.

✓ Maximise Your Marks

To gain higher marks, you need to show that you understand what might be classed as a valid use for illegal drugs. You could refer to the use of cannabis by some elderly people to help themselves.

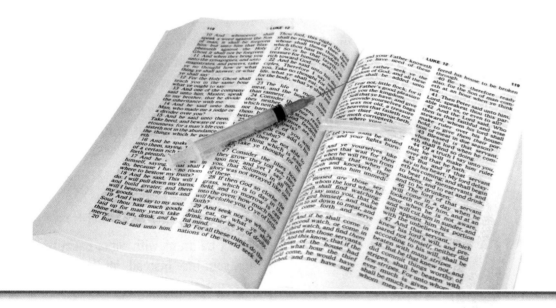

❓ Test Yourself

1. Name two 'Class A' drugs.
2. Explain why drugs are in different classes.
3. List two reasons why drugs are used.
4. How might drug use affect people related to the user?

⭐ Stretch Yourself

1. Explain why China may feel that the death penalty is suitable for drug dealing.
2. Explain why a religious believer may argue against the penalty of death for drug dealing.

Ethics

Alcohol and Tobacco

What are Alcohol and Tobacco?

Alcohol is a drug found in drinks that are only sold to adults in the UK. It is produced during the fermenting of either hops, wheat, barley or fruits.

Tobacco is found in cigarettes and cigars and is not itself a drug. However, it contains nicotine that is a highly addictive drug, even though it is only found in small quantities, approximately 13 mg per cigarette.

UK Drug Law Today

UK law on drugs is very complicated and detailed. For a new drug to be made legal it has to pass many tests. If alcohol or tobacco were to be released today it is likely that neither of them would be legalised by the UK government. There are a number of reasons for this:

- They are both very addictive.
- They cause long term health damage.
- People addicted to either alcohol or tobacco put a huge strain on the **National Health Service**.

Effects of Alcohol

Alcohol acts like an antidepressant. This means that it makes you feel better about yourself for a short period of time and often leads to people acting in ways they wouldn't normally do. It has many short term and long term effects on the body.

✓ Maximise Your Marks

Make sure that you can list at least two ways in which alcohol consumption might help the body and two ways in which it can damage the body.

The Religious View

The **Christian** view about alcohol use varies from denomination to denomination. Almost all believe that it is wrong to get drunk.

"It isn't smart to get drunk! Drinking makes a fool of you and leads to fights."
(Proverbs, chapter 20, verse 1)

They believe this is mainly because you lose control of your body when you are drunk and this is against the will of the Holy Spirit.

"Don't be drunk with wine, because that will ruin your life. Instead, let the Holy Spirit fill and control you."
(Ephesians chapter 5, verse 18)

However, drinking in moderation raises different views.

Methodists believe that alcohol can be drunk occasionally, but almost always not brought into church, even for **communion**.

Roman Catholics generally believe that alcohol consumption is fine in moderation. Most wine used during communion will be alcoholic.

The Religious View (cont.)

Orthodox Christians do not encourage the use of alcohol as they suggest that its continued use often leads to problems in life such as the breakdown of relationships. Therefore alcohol is not generally consumed by Orthodox Christians, but this is not an absolute rule.

Jews follow a similar teaching to that of most Christians, frowning upon being drunk but allowing the consumption of alcohol – in accordance with the **Proverbs** passage above.

In **Sikhism**, the rules regarding the consumption of alcohol are very strict. They are instructed that all forms of alcohol are to be avoided, even though the following passage only refers to wine, and that no good work will absolve anyone from this.

"O Kabeer! Those mortals who consume marijuana, fish and wine – no matter what pilgrimages, fasts and rituals they follow, they will all go to hell." (SGGS, Ang 1377)

Muslims argue that getting drunk is wrong. They also follow the teaching of the Qur'an that forbids alcohol to be present in the mosque. The Qur'an also teaches that a Muslim should not pray whilst they are drunk. However, a Muslim can drink, where state law allows, but only in moderation.

"O ye who believe! Draw not near unto prayer when ye are drunken, till ye know that which ye utter." (Surah 4, verse 43)

Reasons for Smoking

When tobacco was brought onto the UK market, very little was known about the effects that it would have on a human body. Many people began to smoke because they saw smoking in adverts and films and it became something that people did socially. However, in the last twenty years knowledge of the damage caused has greatly increased yet new people still start smoking, this is despite cigarette packets featuring warnings that smoking causes death!

So why do people still smoke?
- The majority of people who smoke are addicted and can't stop.
- Younger people will often start smoking if their parents smoke.
- Many people begin smoking because their friends smoke.

✓ Maximise Your Marks

Explain your own view on alcohol and comment on how its use has changed in the last twenty years. You then need to study the links that your views have with any religion of your choosing.

❓ Test Yourself

1. What is the addictive drug in tobacco?
2. What are the legal ages that you can buy tobacco and alcohol in the UK?
3. Give one reason why a religious believer might disagree with the use of alcohol.
4. List two health issues that alcohol can cause and two that tobacco can cause.

⭐ Stretch Yourself

1. 'Smoking is worse than drinking because it affects more people.' List the arguments for and against this statement and your opinion.
2. Explain why it might be better to never drink or smoke than it is to plan to do it only once.

Practice Questions

Complete these exam-style questions to test your understanding. Check your answers on page 94. You may wish to answer these questions on a separate piece of paper.

1 Describe the teachings that a religious believer might use to support their attitudes towards racial prejudice. (4)

2 Describe religious attitudes towards fertility treatment and the use of human embryos. (4)

3 Describe religious teachings about the value of human life. (3)

4 Explain how a religious believer might respond to the terminally ill who say they want to end their lives. (3)

5 Explain how religious teaching could influence the attitude of a religious believer towards fertility treatment. (4)

....

....

....

....

....

6 For all of the following questions, explain whether you agree with the statement. You must then give reasons to support your answer and show that you have thought about different points of view. You must refer to the teachings of at least one religion in your answer.

a) "Animals were made by God for humans to use, so using them for testing is ok." (4)

....

....

....

....

b) "Only God has the right to end life." (4)

....

....

....

....

c) "It is impossible to treat all people equally." (4)

....

....

....

....

....

Ethics

How well did you do?

| 0–17 | Try again | 18–21 | Getting there | 22–25 | Good work | 26–30 | Excellent! |

Notes

Answers

Foundations of Religion

Pages 4–5 Judaism and Christianity
Test Yourself Answers

1. **a)** The wise men were the key visitors in Matthew.
   b) The shepherds were the key visitors in Luke.
2. Pontius Pilate is important because he had to sanction any action against Jesus.
   The High Priest (and Sanhedrin) sought Jesus' death.
   Peter and the disciples deserted Jesus.

Stretch Yourself Answers

1.

Against	For
• Jesus wasn't dead.	• The soldiers made sure he was dead.
• He revived in the tomb.	• If he revived, he couldn't get out of the tomb and into town.
• His body was stolen (authorities/disciples).	• Guards would prevent death.
• People saw a ghost.	• Ghosts aren't physical and don't eat fish.
• It was all a lie.	• The disciples wouldn't die for a lie.

Pages 6–7 Islam and Sikhism
Test Yourself Answers

1. Allah revealed His message to Muhammad through the angel Gabriel in a cave.
   Because he couldn't read, Muhammad had to recite until he memorised Allah's words.
   Subsequently, he taught this message to his followers.
2. The five 'K's are:
   Kesh: uncut hair
   Kangha: a comb
   Kara: a steel bracelet
   Kacchha: practical shorts
   Kirpan: a steel sword
   They are important for Sikhs because they are a visible and outward sign of their faith.

Stretch Yourself Answers

1. While it is correct that Sikhism has united many believers into one faith, it is also true that greater tension and division exists as a result of antagonism between the three faiths.

Pages 8–9 Beliefs
Test Yourself Answers

1. **a)** They are all monotheistic.
   b) Judaism/Christianity/Islam all believe that heaven and hell awaits everyone after judgement has taken place. Sikhism teaches that reincarnation occurs and souls return in a new physical existence.

Stretch Yourself Answers

1. Good examples would be: Judaism – Deuteronomy 6:4 'Hear, O Israel: The LORD our God, the LORD is one.' Christianity – Matthew 22:37 'Jesus replied: "Love the Lord your God with all your heart and with all your soul and with all your mind."'

Pages 10–11 Jewish and Christian Holy Books
Test Yourself Answers

1. To answer this question, you need to focus on the major prophets:
   • Amos' message was about judgement.
   • Hosea focused on God's relationship with His people.
   • Isaiah encouraged the people and looked forward to the Messiah.
   • Jeremiah warned the people about judgement and reliance on God.
   • Ezekiel saw strange visions and taught about renewal.
2. Peter was the leader of the Church in Jerusalem. Paul took the Gospel to the Gentiles.

Stretch Yourself Answers

1. For example: **Mark** – perhaps an eye-witness, earliest to be written (AD 65) [although some would argue for proto-Luke], preached the Gospel, got information from Peter, etc.

Pages 12–13 Muslim and Sikh Holy Books
Test Yourself Answers

1. **a)** Jews
   Respect is shown by hand-writing each scroll. The scrolls are kept in the Ark and covered in fine cloth. Worshippers stand when the scrolls are brought in. A yad is used to avoid touching the text. When it can no longer be used, a scroll is buried.
   b) Christians
   Respect is shown by closely studying the Bible. When being read, it is placed on a Lectern.
   c) Muslims
   Respect is shown by washing before touching the Qur'an. It is wrapped in fine cloth and kept in a clean place on the highest shelf. Muslims behave well in its presence.
   d) Sikhs
   Respect is shown by bathing before touching the book. It is covered in silk cloth and kept in a bed in its own room. Sikhs carry it above their heads and present it with gifts. It is always read before making important decisions.

Stretch Yourself Answers

1. **a)** The answer would contain explanations about learning about their faith, guidance about living, listening to God's message today, etc.
   b) The answer would include personal experiences of respect outlined in the 'Test Yourself' answers (above).

Pages 14–15 The Gospels
Test Yourself Answers

1. Matthew is composed of Mark, 'Q' and his own source (M).
   Mark was probably an eye-witness and got information from Peter.
   Luke used Mark, 'Q' and his own source (Mary?).
2. No birth stories are included and there is a very short resurrection account.
3. Teaching material in Matthew and Luke not in Mark.

Stretch Yourself Answers

1. A good example of this would be how **Luke's** Gentile background led him to explain Jewish ideas, practices and scriptures for his readers. His life as a doctor can be seen in his treatment of various miracles.

Pages 16–17 Jewish and Christian Holy Buildings
Test Yourself Answers

1. **a)** The ner tamid is the light above the Ark. The Bimah is the raised platform. The parochet is the curtain before the Ark. The Ark contains the scrolls. The menorah is the seven-armed candle holder. The Star of David is often found in stained glass windows.
   b) The altar is where the communion is presented. The pulpit is where the sermon is preached. The lectern is where the Bible is read. The font holds the holy water for baptism. Stained glass windows often tell Bible stories. People cross themselves with water from the holy water stoup. Candles represent light coming into the world.

Stretch Yourself Answers

1. **a)** The ner tamid represents the presence of God. The parochet represents the curtain in the Temple. The Ark represents the Ark of the Covenant.
   b) The font represents baptism. The altar represents the high place of sacrifice. The pulpit represents the centrality of the preached word of God.

Pages 18–19 Muslim and Sikh Holy Buildings
Test Yourself Answers

1. **a)** The mihrab is a niche in the wall facing Mecca. The mimbar are steps where the Imam stands. The dome represents the universe. The minaret is the tower from which the call to prayer is issued.

b) The Takht is the raised platform. The flag flies outside the gurdwara. There are four doors into each gurdwara. The palki is where the Granth is placed. Karah Parshad is the ritual pudding.

Stretch Yourself Answers

1. A correct answer would contain explanations about visual reminders, non-verbal communication of important ideas, focus points to aid concentration, helpful aids for the non-literate, etc.

Pages 20–21 Answers to Practice Questions

1. Churches are often shaped like a cross. *(2 marks)* This separates the congregation from the leader of the worship *(1 mark)* and provides special places for the Bible (lectern), *(1 mark)* for the sermon to be preached from (pulpit) etc. *(1 mark)*
2. The Bible is split into New Testament and Old Testament, *(1 mark)* the Old Testament is before the birth of Christ *(1 mark)* and the New Testament features His birth and the life of the early Church after His ascension. *(1 mark)* Primarily, the New Testament teaches about how Christians should live their lives *(1 mark)* and teaches them the history of their religion. *(1 mark)*
3. It helps to understand how the believer should act, *(1 mark)* it informs them of the key beliefs of their religion, *(1 mark)* can help them feel as though they belong to the religion, *(1 mark)* and can help show how the religion is connected to other religions in the world. *(2 marks)*
4. Guides them in their everyday lives, *(1 mark)* can provide them with answers to important questions, *(1 mark)* guide them as to what they should do in their future, *(1 mark)* teaches them the history of their religion *(1 mark)* and may show them how others have struggled with similar issues to those they are experiencing. *(1 mark)*
5. They were written from different points of view, *(2 marks)* they were written for different audiences, *(1 mark)* and they were probably informed by different eye-witnesses. *(2 marks)*
6. a) For – An all-loving God would want as many people as possible to go to heaven, *(1 mark)* this would be the ultimate application of the golden rule. *(1 mark)* Against – Most religions teach that they are correct and others are not, *(1 mark)* Jesus was clear that He was the only way in which someone could enter heaven. *(1 mark)*
   b) For – Taught by their religions that this is true, *(1 mark)* a religious believer can often point to times in their life when the words from the book have appeared to have more meaning that the words of just a normal book. *(1 mark)* Against – It is just a book; *(1 mark)* they can't all be right. *(1 mark)*
   c) For – God is omnipresent, everywhere all of the time, so I can worship him anywhere. *(1 mark)* I can pray and read scriptures at any time. *(1 mark)* Against – Scriptures teach that it is important to spend time in fellowship with other believers. *(1 mark)* Holy buildings help people to worship as there are much less distractions to the religious believer. *(1 mark)*

Religious Practice

Pages 22–23 Jewish and Christian Worship
Test Yourself Answers

1. Reading scriptures, singing hymns, praying, preaching sermons, chanting and bowing are elements of worship that can be found in most Jewish and Christian faiths.
2. Attitude to scriptures, methods of praying, leadership and different holy days are the main points of difference. They exist largely because of cultural and historical difference.
3. Jewish worship is led by a rabbi. Christian worship is led by a vicar/priest. Muslim worship is led by an Imam. Sikh worship can be led by any Sikh.

Stretch Yourself Answers

1. The answer would contain references to scriptures, prayer, singing, sermons, etc. The differences would focus on clothing, separation of sexes, use of scriptures, language, etc. The differences would take into account language, tradition, culture, etc.

Pages 24–25 Muslim and Sikh Worship
Test Yourself Answers

1. The main elements are reading scripture, listening to sermons and praying.
2. The main preparations for worship are removing shoes, covering heads and wudu.

Stretch Yourself Answers

1. The answer should include references to singing hymns, offering gifts, bowing, praying and reading and chanting scriptures. These would be important because of the reverence Sikhs have for scripture, etc.

Pages 26–27 Attitudes to Prayer
Test Yourself Answers

1. Adoration, Confession, Thanksgiving and Supplication are the main types of Christian prayer. Special mention should be made of Salat and Rak'ah in Muslim prayer.
2. Prayer is important because of communicating with God, seeking guidance, praising God, supplication and closeness with God.

Stretch Yourself Answers

1. a) The answer should include: any time, set times, in church, by themselves, with others, etc.
   b) The answer should include: anywhere, in church, at home, etc.
   c) The answer should include: listening to God, communicating with God, petitioning God and praising God, etc.

Pages 28–29 Pilgrimage
Test Yourself Answers

1. Jews might visit Jerusalem, Masada, Yad Vashem and Mount Sinai.
   Christians might visit Israel, Rome, Lourdes, Canterbury, Walsingham, etc.
   Muslims must visit Mecca (Hajj).
   Sikhs might visit the Golden Temple at Amritsar.
2. Jews have a deep reverence for the remains of the Temple.
   Christians visit because of Jesus' death and resurrection.
   Muslims visit the Dome of the Rock because of the Hijra.

Stretch Yourself Answers

1. The answer should include references to learning more about their faith, God and themselves, etc.

Pages 30–31 Jewish and Christian Rites of Passage
Test Yourself Answers

1. For Jews the rites of passage are Brit Milah, Bar/Bat Mitzvah, Marriage and Death.
   For Christians they are Infant baptism, Confirmation, Marriage and Death.

Stretch Yourself Answers

1. The answer should include references starting with the covenant between God and Abram (Abraham), God's demands and promises and it being a sign in the flesh of the covenant.

Pages 32–33 Muslim and Sikh Rites of Passage
Test Yourself Answers

1. Sikhs welcome a baby into the faith by worshipping together. Hymns are sung and scriptures read. Prayers are said and Karah Parshad is distributed. Amrit is placed on the baby's lips. The Granth is opened at random: the first letter on the page becomes the first letter of the name. Kaur or Singh is added to the name.
2. Seven days after birth.

Stretch Yourself Answers

1. Arguments for would include families uniting, the importance of older wisdom, tradition, etc. Arguments against would include the importance of free will and choice, Western tradition, etc.
2. Ceremonies depend on what is expected after death, the existence of heaven and hell or reincarnation.

Pages 34–35 Jewish and Christian Festivals
Test Yourself Answers

1. The events and foods are:
   Matzo – unleavened bread
   Lamb bone – Paschal lamb
   Roasted egg – sacrifice
   Bitter herbs – suffering in slavery
   Lettuce – new life
   Salt water – tears in slavery
   Charoset – mortar for buildings
   Wine – liberty and joy
   Elijah's cup – promised of the Messiah
2. Forty days

Stretch Yourself Answers

1. Palm Sunday is about expectation. Maundy Thursday focuses on the Last Supper and foot washing (sadness and service). Good Friday is concerned with the crucifixion of Jesus (sadness and sacrifice). Easter Day recalls the resurrection of Jesus (joy and celebration).

Pages 36–37 Muslim and Sikh Festivals
Test Yourself Answers
1. **Ramadan and Eid-ul-Fitr**
   a) During the ninth month, Muslims must fast during daylight hours. At the end of Ramadan, Muslims celebrate Eid-ul-Fitr to thank Allah for his strength to complete the fast.
   b) Ramadan recalls the giving of the Qur'an.
   c) Eid-ul-Fitr is celebrated with special services, processions, new clothes, gifts, cards and a special Eid meal. Eid ul Adha is a four-day festival which celebrates Abraham's (Ibrahim's) willingness to sacrifice his son. Muslims sacrifice a sheep which is distributed between family, friends and the poor. Presents are exchanged and there are special prayers.

   Diwali
   a) Diwali is the Festival of Lights.
   b) It celebrates the release from prison of the sixth guru, Guru Hargobind and 52 other princes in 1619.
   c) Homes are decorated, new clothes bought, gifts given and special worship conducted.

   Baisakhi
   a) This is the New Year festival.
   b) It celebrates the creation of the Khalsa by Guru Gobind Singh in 1699.
   c) As part of the celebrations, it is a very popular day for Sikhs to be baptised into the Sikh brotherhood.

Stretch Yourself Answers
1. Festivals mark major points in the life of a religion and usually have a foundation in historical events. They provide an opportunity to celebrate the birth, life or death of the founder or revered leader of their faith.

Pages 38–39 Jewish and Christian Views on Afterlife
Test Yourself Answers
1. For those who do, entry to heaven depends on keeping the Torah.
2. Images associated with heaven might include being with God, happiness, angels, joy, clouds, reward, pleasure, etc. Images associated with hell might include suffering, Satan, punishment, fire, unhappiness, etc.

Stretch Yourself Answers
1. Catholics find the idea of Purgatory important because it offers hope for non-believers, a second chance, cleansing of sins, final entry to heaven, escape from hell, etc.

Pages 40–41 Muslim and Sikh Views on Afterlife
Test Yourself Answers
1. a) For Jews, Christians and Muslims they are places of reward and punishment (different descriptions of each/different methods of entry). For Sikhs they are a state of mind or a position in society on Earth.
   b) For Jews it is about keeping the Law and the coming of Messiah. For Christians it involves 'commitment' to Jesus. For Muslims it is about submission to the will of Allah (Qur'an).
2. For Jews it means the Coming of Messiah and Yahweh being a just judge. For Christians it involves the Day of Judgement and the Second Coming (Parousia). For Muslims it is the Day of Judgement (Day of Resurrection).

Stretch Yourself Answers
1. The answer should include a description of the cycle of life and the transmigration of the soul, dependent on Karma. Escape from reincarnation would involve an explanation of union with God through true repentance and dedication.

Pages 42–43 Answers to Practice Questions
1. To be in a place where they know a significant member of their religion has been, to feel closer to God, (2 marks) as penance for something they have done wrong, (1 mark) because their religion teaches them to (Five Pillars of Islam). (2 marks)
2. All holy books are used in many different ways. Many readings are made from them, (1 mark) Sikhs have to sit below the Guru Granth Sahib, (1 mark) teachings are given from the books during services, (1 mark) songs may be sung from the books or songs may be written based on passages from any one of the books. (1 mark)
3. A believer may feel that prayer provides support for them in their lives. (1 mark) It can be seen as giving them the chance to talk to their God. (1 mark) A believer can thank God during prayer. (1 mark) They can also praise God and ask for guidance. (1 mark)
4. The ceremony brings a child into the faith. (1 mark) The ceremony lets the parents thank God for their child in a public setting. (1 mark) It also allows the family and friends to make promises over their child in front of God.

(1 mark) The whole of the religious community share in the celebration of the birth. (1 mark) The child is publicly given its name. (1 mark)
5. Pilgrimage can help a believer feel closer to God. (1 mark) It may help to restore their faith. (1 mark) It can help a religious believer to deal with a difficult time in their lives. (1 mark) It can also help them to overcome something that they may have done wrong in the past. (2 marks)
6. A believer can celebrate important events in the history of their religion. (1 mark) A festival provides an opportunity to teach non-believers about the religion. (1 mark) It helps to explain the history of the religion to younger members of the faith. (1 mark) A festival ensures that key parts of the religion's history are not forgotten. (1 mark)
7. a) For – Scripture teaches that God is everywhere, (1 mark) faith is a personal experience between the believer and God. (1 mark) Against – Scripture teaches that meeting together with other believers is important (fellowship), (1 mark) much easier to worship in a holy building as there are less distractions. (1 mark)
   b) For – There is lots of poverty in the world, (1 mark) religion teaches to care for other people. (1 mark) Against – Five Pillars of Islam, personal experience with God, (1 mark) a believer may feel called by God to go on a pilgrimage. (1 mark)
   c) For – All religious believers are climbing the same mountain of faith, (1 mark) it could be linked to Karma and reincarnation. (1 mark) Against – What if there is no God? (1 mark) Jesus said only He was the way to get to heaven not good deeds. (1 mark)

Religious Attitudes

Pages 44–45 Origins of Crime and Punishment
Test Yourself Answers
1. A sin is an act or thought against a god, a crime is an act against the state.
2. The aim of deterrence works by ensuring that the punishments are severe to try and put people off committing the crime.

Stretch Yourself Answers
1. The 10 Commandments may be viewed as being an out-of-date set of rules because not everyone is religious; not all of the commandments are crimes and the commandments are thousands of years old.

Pages 46–47 Views on Crime and Punishment
Test Yourself Answers
1. A Muslim would consider using the death penalty when any of the following have occurred: treason/apostasy, terrorism, piracy of any kind, rape and adultery.
2. Rehabilitation could help someone charged with drug possession. Retribution or restoration may act as a suitable punishment for theft. Deterrence as an aim of punishment may be suitable in cases of rape or murder.
3. Mainly deterrence or rehabilitation, stop people from committing the crime in the first place or help them to stop committing crime.

Stretch Yourself Answers
1. For – stops crime, acts as a deterrent, can be justified if the crime is severe.
   Against – who has the right to end life? Mistaken identity, someone could be forced to commit the crime.

Pages 48–49 Forgiveness
Test Yourself Answers
1. When the victim tells the person that has wronged them that the event is now in the past.
2. In cases of betrayal or extreme crime such as murder.
3. They are taught by their religion that they should and it will influence what happens to them in the afterlife.
4. The first forgiven person sees the example of forgiveness and feels that they should then forgive someone else.

Stretch Yourself Answers
1. No – still have to face earthly consequences, from damaged relationships through to serving time in prison.
2. • Old Testament – eye for an eye, face the punishment that matches the crime committed, then forgiveness can follow.
   • New Testament – based on forgiveness first then the individual can face the punishment.

Pages 50–51 Stewardship
Test Yourself Answers
1. The belief that people are trusted by God to care for the planet.
2. Support a charity, recycle, use renewable energy, use their cars only when they need to, try to cut down on waste.
3. Invest in renewable energy sources, provide more public transport, encourage people to recycle more.
4. Reduces waste, sees items that would be thrown away reused and then stops items that could become something else from being wasted.

Stretch Yourself Answers
1. Both books state that humans are to care for the planet. They both state that the world was created by their God.
2. If something is sustainable then it is managed and controlled to allow it to be used without it running out.

Pages 52–53 Relationships and the Family
Test Yourself Answers
1. To have children, a sign of commitment, because they are in love.
2. Might worship together, follow the teachings of their religion, study scripture.
3. Too expensive, people are getting married for the right reasons, more religious weddings.
4. Provides two parents, a stable home, religions teach that it is right.

Stretch Yourself Answers
1. • For – making promises for the second time, have had sex with someone else.
   • Against – still promises made before God, still could be for all of the right reasons. Can't afford to get married, might not be religious, are happy with their relationship, may have already been married.

Pages 54–55 Poverty and Wealth
Test Yourself Answers
1. UK – not afford all bills or food; Third World – no clothes, no home, no clean water.
2. Debts cancelled, charity work supported, fair price paid for goods.
3. Get distracted from God, could become greedy, might not give enough of it to charity.
4. Loans, natural disasters, because they were born into poverty.

Stretch Yourself Answers
1. Being rich brings complications, can remove a reliance on God, can become greedy.
2. Good – help others, can be used to relieve suffering. Bad – can cause greed and then maybe even war, can take people away from religion.

Pages 56–57 Theodicy
Test Yourself Answers
1. Theodicy is the problem that there is suffering in the world but many people believe that there is an all-loving God.
2. When someone or a group of people feel physical or psychological pain because of the circumstances they are in.
3. Follow the golden rule, strive to end poverty.
4. Because an all-loving God is likely to stop suffering if He exists.

Stretch Yourself Answers
1. No – everyone would be without pain, peace would happen. Yes – seems impossible to have no suffering, how would people appreciate good? Would no suffering actually be heaven?
2. Bring them closer to God, help them to want to help others.

Pages 58–59 Suffering
Test Yourself Answers
1. Types of suffering caused by man include: poverty, disease because of war.
2. Suffering could be overcome if people acted as religions instructed them to and/or if third world debt was ended.
3. Man is not capable of living in a world without suffering in it; history shows this. For example, communism should have made everyone equal but it only needed one person to be greedy for it to stop working.

Stretch Yourself Answers
1. For – God created the universe so created evil, He has the power to stop it but doesn't.
   Against – free will, evil comes from Satan not God, God only allows it to happen so that we have consequences to our actions.

2. Real pain can make an individual doubt the existence of a God, reduce their quality of life, make them angry and could lead them to push those that love them away.

Pages 60–61 Answers to Practice Questions
1. All religions believe that they are called by God to care for those around them. *(1 mark)* Describe the parable of 'The Good Samaritan' and how it shows love. *(2 marks)* Comment that religions teach that we should love one another regardless of differences. *(1 mark)*
2. God created the world so religious believers are trusted with taking care of it. *(2 marks)* This is called stewardship. *(1 mark)* We must ensure that we protect the Earth for the generations that follow us. *(1 mark)* If we act out of love then we will protect plants and animals. *(1 mark)*
3. 'Free will' is the understanding that we all have the ability to make our own choices. *(1 mark)* If we were not able to choose then God would have made robots. *(1 mark)* For a Sikh, we cause it to happen through our actions in line with Karma. *(1 mark)*
4. Each religion teaches its followers that they should help those poorer than themselves. *(1 mark)* A charity can help in ways that a religious believer might not be able to by themselves. *(1 mark)* A charity may help to promote the key values of the religion. *(1 mark)*
5. They would probably advise against divorce in most cases. *(1 mark)* They would encourage the couple to seek counselling. *(1 mark)* They would help them to see the value of the promises they made during the wedding ceremony. *(1 mark)* A religious believer may advise a couple to spend some time apart first and try and help them to find out what their God wants them to do. *(1 mark)*
6. A religious believer could ensure that they recycle the waste that can be saved. *(1 mark)* They could encourage others to do the same by setting an example. *(1 mark)* A believer could also think about the energy that they use and not waste it. *(1 mark)* Through donations, a believer could support charities that work to protect the environment. *(1 mark)* Finally, a believer could vote for politicians who believe what they do in terms of protecting the planet. *(1 mark)*
7. a) For – The death penalty is likely to make people think twice before committing a crime. It will definitely stop people from committing the crime again. *(1 mark)*
   Against – In many cases an act of murder is a crime of passion. *(1 mark)* It has been shown not to work in countries such as China. *(1 mark)* The 10 Commandments teach do not murder. *(1 mark)*
   b) For – There are cases of suffering all over the world. *(1 mark)* It could be argued that an all-loving God would not allow suffering to happen. *(1 mark)*
   Against – God allows all of us to choose how we behave (free will). *(1 mark)* Man is the cause of most of the suffering that we see around the world. *(1 mark)*
   c) For – Scriptures teach that sex should be within marriage. *(1 mark)* It could be argued that children are probably best taken care of inside a marriage. *(1 mark)*
   Against – Not everyone is religious so should not have to follow religious rules. *(1 mark)* A couple may choose to have sex without the commitment of marriage. *(1 mark)*

Ethics

Pages 62–63 Sanctity of Life
Test Yourself Answers
1. Given by God, only God can end it, God created the universe.
2. Conceived in rape, crimes committed.
3. Abortion, euthanasia, embryology, murder, the death penalty.
4. Active euthanasia and murder is against the law. Also there is no death penalty in the UK.

Stretch Yourself Answers
1. Changes in the abortion laws, not to allow it until after 14 days in line with Church's teaching on embryology.
2. Different religions and not all people are religious, therefore very different opinions exist.

Pages 64–65 When Does Life Begin?
Test Yourself Answers
1. God is present at the start.
2. The quickening.
3. At birth.
4. Zygote, foetus, embryo.

Stretch Yourself Answers

1.

Similarities	Differences
• Each religion believes that God creates life • Each religion believes God makes humans different from the rest of creation by giving them a soul • In terms of abortion, they hold that ultimately the mother's life is more important and should be protected	• Many Christians and Jews believe that life starts at conception • Muslims believe that life starts at 120 days (the quickening) • Members of the Church of England are more likely to allow abortions than a Roman Catholic

2. The quote 'an embryo is only the potential for life' could prompt a variety of different views, including:
   Many religious believers think that an embryo is not potential but is life itself, whether it starts at conception or later at 120 days. The word potential is not clear and does not really differentiate between what is life and what isn't. In terms of a premature birth, when the baby may not be fully developed, it is difficult to then argue whether it is a full life or still a potential for life until its development is complete.

Pages 66–67 In Vitro Fertilisation
Test Yourself Answers
1. AID – donor sperm; AIH – sperm from husband.
2. If AID is used the children will not be living or in contact with their biological father. If AIH is used, the expense and potential multiple births may cause problems within families.
3. Multiple eggs are used as they increase the chance of pregnancy.
4. Surrogacy may be seen as a bad thing, as the child will end up living with its non-biological mother and it could be seen (religiously speaking) as adultery.

Stretch Yourself Answers
1. A child born through AID will be growing up without one of its biological parents. This may lead them to question who their father is and promote a desire to find out in later life. This may cause heartache in the family. However, it allows couples who cannot have a child to begin a family. IVF through AID also helps the couple themselves to have a baby and this child may go on to become a blessing to those around them.
2. A religious believer might be against the use of embryos in scientific testing because they believe that life is given by God and that humans should not 'play God' in the process of birth.

Pages 68–69 Abortion
Test Yourself Answers
1. Premature ending of a pregnancy.
2. Christians think that abortions should be avoided because they can be classed as murder; the embryo is created by God.
3. Some Christians allow abortion up to 14 days; Muslims up to 120 days in most cases. All religions except Judaism would consider abortion to protect the life of the mother.

Stretch Yourself Answers
1. Advantages – In all cases it is the woman who has to carry the pregnancy and endure the pain of child birth. In the early stages of the baby's life it is its mother with whom they form the closet bond and if the mother did not want the pregnancy then the child may be neglected.
   Disadvantages – The will of the father is largely ignored. Even if he would be happy to bring the child up as a single parent, the mother's wishes may prevent him from doing this. The mother may not be of sound mind and may regret the decision she makes in the future if she is not given enough support or guidance.

Pages 70–71 Views on Abortion
Test Yourself Answers
1. A pro-choice believer would be in favour of abortion.
2. Most religious believers are likely to be pro-life supporters.

Stretch Yourself Answers
1. For – The woman should have the ability to make choices about her body. Abortions should be allowed as they can protect the health of the pregnant woman in certain circumstances.
   Against – The embryo is already a life and should be protected. Abortions can be used as a form of contraception.

Pages 72–73 Euthanasia
Test Yourself Answers
1. Euthanasia is legal in the UK when it is passive – the removal of treatment.
2. A medical professional – a doctor.
3. Caring for someone when they truly need help is the best alternative to euthanasia.
4. The term 'playing God' means trying to act in a way that might be unnatural and perhaps going against the wishes of God in a medical environment.

Stretch Yourself Answers
1.

Arguments in favour of euthanasia	Arguments against euthanasia
• It allows the person who is suffering to end their pain • It ensures that someone who is physically unable to commit suicide still has the right to end their life • Euthanasia can also bring relief to the family of someone with a terminal illness	• Many religious believers think that their God is the only one who has the right to take life (sanctity of life) • The hospice movement provides available alternative • Members of the Church of England are more likely to allow euthanasia than a Roman Catholic

2.

Arguments in favour of hospices	Arguments against hospices
• It provides a better quality of life • A hospice can also help the family of the person who is suffering, by providing chances for fun and trips that would otherwise not be possible • It can help the family explain to the child what is happening to them and what is going to happen	• Whatever work it does, the hospice cannot save the child's life • It could be argued that a hospice is prolonging the agony that euthanasia could bring to an end • The child will still continue to feel pain

Pages 74–75 Animal Rights
Test Yourself Answers
1. Vivisection is the testing of products or materials on animals.
2. Religions are more likely to support animal testing when it is used for medical reasons.
3. Animal testing might not be helpful because animals and humans are so different.
4. Two reasons why a religious believer may disagree with animal testing are: God created animals for humans to look after; and animal testing involves unnecessary cruelty.

Stretch Yourself Answers
1. Some Sikhs choose to become vegetarian to show respect for animals and God's creation; also animals play a part in the reincarnation cycle of life.
2. Someone might object to eating meat because of the cruelty inherent in the raising and killing of animals; it is less efficient to eat meat than crops; may not like the taste; and/or their parents are vegetarian so the individual is used to living in a vegetarian environment.

Pages 76–77 War and Peace
Test Yourself Answers
1. 'Jihad' only applies for Muslims and 'Just War' is primarily followed by Christians.
2. The three strongest reasons for war may include: to stop suffering; to defend a religion; and to protect another country.
3. War may not be a bad thing because it can end dictatorships, allow more freedom and/or maintain a culture or religion.

Stretch Yourself Answers
1. Wars cost lots of money to fight but can also boost an economy and provide jobs. In some cases, wars may bring about a more equal distribution of wealth or land (some would argue that is what is happening in Israel and Palestine). It can also be argued that wars sometimes have to be fought to bring about long term peace.
2. Here, you could refer to any of the following wars: Afghanistan, Sierra Leone, Rwanda, Iraq, etc. As an example, the war in Rwanda was a civil war. Many civilians lost their lives and were massacred in large numbers. The government was overthrown and many western people living in the country left. This partly led to the country being left in a very poor state with many Rwandans needing humanitarian aid.

Pages 78–79 Views on War and Peace
Test Yourself Answers
1. Someone might choose to be a conscientious objector because of their religion.
2. 1961.

Stretch Yourself Answers
1. A religious believer is likely to believe that their God created life. They may also believe that only God has the right to take life. They may argue that diplomacy should always be used first.

Pages 80–81 Prejudice and Discrimination
Test Yourself Answers
1. Racism, sexism, poverty, discrimination based upon religion, discrimination based upon sexual preference.
2. Discrimination might be shown through verbal attacks, bullying and/or denying someone a job.
3. Problems caused by discrimination may include: dividing a community, leading to suffering and/or causing war(s).
4. Discrimination could be dealt with by people spending time talking to each other, educating children in school, and/or stronger laws.

Stretch Yourself Answers
1. In this question a selection of people you can discuss are as follows; Martin Luther King Junior, Mother Teresa, Nelson Mandela, Muhatma Ghandi. Martin Luther King led America to bring about equality for the black population during the 1960s. He argued for peaceful protests and boycotts to force the government to change the laws. Rosa Parks was influential in her stance against the treatment of blacks on buses by refusing to give up her seat. King was ultimately assassinated for his beliefs and his work.
2. Many religions have historically treated women differently to men. In the Roman Catholic Church, women are still prohibited from becoming senior figures in the Church. Each religion also argues that their beliefs system is correct. This means that they have to state that other religions are wrong in their beliefs.

Pages 82–83 Drugs
Test Yourself Answers
1. Class A drugs include: heroin, cocaine, LSD.
2. Because of the affects that they have on the body and the value that they have when being sold.
3. Reasons may include that drugs are used to 'escape', to ease depression, to ease pain and/or peer pressure.
4. People related to a drug user may have their property stolen to fund the drug user's habit and/or their family often end up having to care for the drug user.

Stretch Yourself Answers
1. China may feel that the death penalty is suitable for drug dealing because such a severe penalty would stop drug use from happening and certainly deter drug dealers.
2. A religious believer may argue against the penalty of death for drug dealing because in their view only God should end life; it is not a proportionate punishment; cases of mistaken identity have been known so the wrong person has undergone the death penalty; and/or cases where someone is forced to deal in drugs would mean that the wrong person is being punished.

Pages 84–85 Alcohol and Tobacco
Test Yourself Answers
1. Nicotine.
2. Both are now 18.

3. Alcohol damages the body; there are teachings in scripture(s) that are against drinking; and/or when drunk you often lose control of how you act.
4. Alcohol – liver disease, heart disease. Tobacco – various forms of cancer, asthma.

Stretch Yourself Answers
1.

Arguments in favour	Arguments against
• Passive smoking damages the health of people around the smoker • If someone starts smoking cigarettes it can lead to them using harder drugs	• More young people drink alcohol than smoke • Drinking excessive amounts of alcohol can lead to violence

2. Both alcohol and cigarettes are very addictive. Similarly, too much alcohol consumed in one go can kill.

Pages 86–87 Answers to Practice Questions
1. Scriptures teach their followers to treat all humans equally. (1 mark) Jesus spent time with people of all races and backgrounds. (1 mark) Christians could use the parable of the Good Samaritan to show love for others. (1 mark) Racism should be avoided as it can lead to war. (1 mark)
2. Most religious believers would agree with the use of IVF through AIH. (1 mark) However, most religious believers disagree with IVF through AID. (1 mark) Many religious believers would argue that embryology is wrong if they believe that life starts at conception. (1 mark) However, those who believe that life starts later, like Muslims, may allow it. (1 mark)
3. Religious believers believe that their God created all life. (1 mark) Therefore, only He should take it away. (1 mark) This means that in many cases euthanasia and abortion are wrong. (1 mark)
4. They would advise against euthanasia. (1 mark) A believer would also try to convince them to take a place in a hospice as an alternative. (1 mark) Time could be spent to teach them about the believer's religion in a sensitive way. (1 mark)
5. If the religious believer believes life begins at conception, then they may think IVF is wrong as life is being formed outside of the womb. (2 marks) If they believe life starts at 120 days or at birth they may not have the same problem. (1 mark) All believers could argue though, that IVF is like 'playing God'. (1 mark)
6. a) For – Genesis 2 gives the Christian and Jewish account of creation, stating that man was made separate to all other creatures. (1 mark) The passage also states that humans are made in 'God's image'. (1 mark)
   Against – A belief in reincarnation will see greater value placed upon the life of animals. (1 mark) Eating meat can be seen as a waste of resources as it is more economical and better for the environment to not eat meat. (1 mark)
   b) For – Sanctity of life teaches that God created life so only He can take it away. (1 mark) Questions could be raised as to who has the right to decide when someone dies or not. (1 mark)
   Against – As not everyone is religious then the argument for the sanctity of life loses value. (1 mark) Individual people should be able to choose when to end their own life. (1 mark)
   c) For – All religions teach a different set of beliefs and ways to live. (1 mark) Humans naturally see differences in each other's appearances. (1 mark)
   Against – If all people applied the principle of the Good Samaritan then equality could be achieved. (1 mark) True equality may be what the afterlife is like. (1 mark)

Index

Index